T0246962

DEVOTIONS
& PRAYERS

for a

"NO REGRETS"
LIFE

MARILEE PARRISH

DEVOTIONS & PRAYERS

for a

"NO REGRETS" LIFE

INSPIRATION &
ENCOURAGEMENT
FOR TEEN GIRLS

BARBOUR
PUBLISHING

Published by Barbour Publishing, Inc., 1810 Barbour Drive, Uhrichsville, Ohio 44683, www.barbourbooks.com

Our mission is to inspire the world with the life-changing message of the Bible.

Member of the
Evangelical Christian
Publishers Association

Printed in China.

INTRODUCTION

True story: I've had plenty of regrets in my life. I had to learn things in what felt to me like the hardest way possible. I spent decades of my life doing everything my own way. And life was hard.

Midway through my thirties, I came to the very end of myself. With nowhere else to go but to call out to the heavens for help, I found Jesus. Or, more accurately, He found me. I came to realize that He'd never let me go. He saw me. He knew me. He pursued me like the shepherd in the Bible who left the ninety-nine to go looking for the lost one. I was that lost one.

As I began to process all that I'd done, God became very real to me. He showed me that I was "washed" (1 Corinthians 6:11). His love covered all my mistakes, failures, and sins. He had overwhelming grace for me. He lovingly called me into relationship with Him and showed me a new and different way.

Through the pages of this book, you'll hear some Bible stories and some contemporary stories of choices big and small that went wrong and how you can learn from these mistakes so you don't go down that hard road yourself.

I pray that this book encourages you to approach God's throne of grace with confidence to find mercy and grace right when you need it (Hebrews 4:16)!

Love and blessings as you read,
MariLee

WHAT SOME OF YOU WERE

*And that is what some of you were. But you were washed,
you were sanctified, you were justified in the name of
the Lord Jesus Christ and by the Spirit of our God.*
1 Corinthians 6:11 NIV

If you look in your Bible at 1 Corinthians 6:7–11, you're going to see quite a list of regrets and sins. Some may even seem shocking to you. But here's the thing: you might find some things you've struggled with yourself in that list. Have you ever been greedy? Have you ever put something else before God, making it an idol (think smartphone maybe)? If we look deep into our hearts, we've probably done something to put ourselves on that list.

Joe came to our Bible study. He had been rejected by some people in his last church because he shared his deepest shame with them in an attempt to be set free. They judged him harshly and turned on him instead. He was broken and insecure, believing lies that he deserved to be alone and unloved.

As we spent time with Joe, 1 Corinthians 6:11 is the verse that kept popping up over and over again. Instead of agreeing with Joe's assessment of himself and his past, God wanted us to see him as washed clean so that Joe would begin believing it himself. Joe had repented of his sin, and so God's words were true of him.

At the end of our small group curriculum, we were directed to write large note cards with each participant's name on them and to ask God for something to say to each person. The Holy

Spirit urged me to write 1 Corinthians 6:11 on Joe's card: "And that is what some of you were. But you were washed. . . ." I included the whole verse on the card.

The New Living Translation says, "Some of you were once like that. But you were cleansed; you were made holy; you were made right with God by calling on the name of the Lord Jesus Christ and by the Spirit of our God."

Joe was on that list in 1 Corinthians 6. But he was washed. He had called on the name of Jesus, and God wanted him to be set free.

Is there something in your life that needs to be washed? Is there a place in your heart that needs to be set free? Maybe you've had a lot of regrets in your past that are holding you back. Jesus wants to make you right with God. Will you let Him?

Jesus, I want to be washed clean. I bring my list of failures and regrets and ask that You set me free. And help me point others to the hope that You offer in our brokenness.

DO YOU WANT TO GET WELL?

*Here a great number of disabled people used to lie—
the blind, the lame, the paralyzed. One who was there had
been an invalid for thirty-eight years. When Jesus saw him
lying there and learned that he had been in this condition
for a long time, he asked him, "Do you want to get well?"*
JOHN 5:3–6 NIV

We talked yesterday of being "washed." And speaking of that,
check out the story in John 5. Many sick and disabled people
would wait around this special pool in the city of Jerusalem
because they believed that if they went into the water after the
waters were stirred up, they would be healed. Jesus saw a man
there who had been paralyzed for thirty-eight years. Guess what
Jesus asked him? "Do you want to get well?"

Doesn't that seem like a strange question to ask someone
who is paralyzed? Why would Jesus say such a thing? Of course
the man would want to get well—wouldn't he? But the truth is
that sometimes people have wounds in their bodies and their
hearts that they like to hold on to. Maybe they are scared to be
or do anything other than what feels "normal" to them—even if
normal means dysfunctional and painful. Or maybe they just don't
know any better until someone shares truth and love with them.

So Jesus asked this man a question that went straight to his
heart: "Do you want to get well?"

The man didn't really answer Jesus' question directly. But
take a look at what happened: "Then Jesus said to him, 'Get

up! Pick up your mat and walk.' At once the man was cured; he picked up his mat and walked" (verses 8–9 NIV).

The Bible says that Jesus went into the temple later and saw this same man whom He had healed. He told the man that he should not return to a life of sin or something worse might happen. Like a life of regret.

So Jesus healed the man at the pool, and after decades of being lame, the man could finally walk. Jesus urged him not to fall back into sin. And that's the thing! That list of sins we talked about yesterday in 1 Corinthians? You can't just talk yourself out of them. After you've been washed, you have to pick up your mat and walk away from that old life. With the help of the Holy Spirit, you have to put big-time boundaries in your life so that you don't fall back into sin.

Do you want to get well?

Jesus, take a look into my heart and help me understand what's going on in there. I believe I want to be well. Will You help me pick up my mat and walk away from everything that You're calling me away from?

HOW TO PICK UP YOUR MAT AND WALK

Jesus told him, "Stand up, pick up your mat,
and walk!" Instantly, the man was healed!
He rolled up his sleeping mat and began walking!
JOHN 5:8–9 NLT

A friend shared an illustration with me that she heard from a pastor. He was talking about boundaries and sin. He said that if your house is right next door to a busy highway, you have to build a big fence between your house and the road so that your kids can safely play in the yard.

It's the same way with sin and regret. If you've gone down a road you regret, you have to put up a big fence so that you're not tempted to go back down that road again.

What does that look like in real life? Here's a real example: Ellie got in big trouble with some friends in a group chat on her phone. She ignored the red flags and majorly crossed the line. What she'd done was wrong, and she knew it. After she confessed to her mom, they chose to get rid of that phone number completely so that some of those people who had been in the group chat wouldn't be able to contact her anymore. She needed a big fence there.

When Jesus washes you clean and tells you to pick up your mat and walk, He wants you to walk away from anything that will cause you regret in the future. He wants you to be free and filled with peace and joy as you live the life He created you for.

But what if it's really hard to pick up your mat and walk away? What if too many feelings and relationships are involved? What if it seems more complicated than anything you've faced before? John 14:26 (AMP) gives us all the encouragement we need: "But the Helper (Comforter, Advocate, Intercessor—Counselor, Strengthener, Standby), the Holy Spirit, whom the Father will send in My name [in My place, to represent Me and act on My behalf], He will teach you all things. And He will help you remember everything that I have told you."

You are not alone as you pick up your mat and walk away. If you've accepted Jesus as your Savior and Lord, you've been given His Spirit to be your helper, your comforter, your counselor, your strengthener, and your guide. If you need a big fence, He'll help you build it. If you need willpower, He'll give you Holy Spirit power.

Jesus, I'm so relieved and thankful that I don't have to do this in my own strength. Your Spirit is alive and at work in me! I can walk away from sin and regret because You help me! You give me the strength and will to move my legs and walk away from the things that are destructive and toward You.

HUMBLE INTERACTIONS

Clothe yourselves with humility toward one another
[tie on the servant's apron], for God is opposed to
the proud [the disdainful, the presumptuous, and He
defeats them], but He gives grace to the humble.

1 PETER 5:5 AMP

My family and I lived in Colorado for fifteen years. Many authors, speakers, and Bible teachers choose to make Colorado their home. One day, a friend asked if I wanted to get together with her and another friend who was the director of a big ministry. I was excited and couldn't wait to glean some wisdom from this Bible teacher. She came to my home, and we had lunch and enjoyed a great afternoon together.

But that very morning, an unexpected friend from our small group came to my house before my afternoon gathering. I knew her story well, and she had worked hard to heal from a childhood of trauma. She hadn't been a Christian very long. This friend was rough around the edges but authentic and real as she daily sought to follow Jesus. She never pretended to be something she wasn't. She was open and honest about her struggles and easy to talk to and share with.

She wanted to come over and catch up. I was thinking that this would be a time of me ministering to her and I would be ministered to later by the Bible teacher. But as we talked about her struggles, I shared one of my own. Can you guess what she asked me? "Do you want to be well?" She shared how that scripture had been changing her and what it could do for me too. We prayed together, and it was powerful!

As I processed my day later in the evening, I was struck by the fact that I was expecting to be blown away by new wisdom from a well-known Bible teacher, but what happened was that my heart was more transformed by the conversation with my diamond-in-the-rough friend.

I am not putting down the Bible teacher; she was awesome! My heart was the problem. I had put this teacher on a pedestal and had slightly elevated my spirituality in comparison to my small-group friend.

Romans 12:16 (AMP) says, "Live in harmony with one another; do not be haughty [conceited, self-important, exclusive], but associate with humble people [those with a realistic self-view]. Do not overestimate yourself."

I learned a lesson in humility that day. I learned that God can teach us through anyone He sends our way. He wants us to be humble in all of our interactions with others—and especially as we lead in areas where He has given us authority.

Lord, help me to be humble in my heart
and in the way I treat everyone around me.
You are the important one around here!

THE LITTLE THINGS

*"The master was full of praise. 'Well done, my good
and faithful servant. You have been faithful in handling
this small amount, so now I will give you many
more responsibilities. Let's celebrate together!' "*

MATTHEW 25:21 NLT

Tyler was a social kid. He loved being in the middle of all the
action. He had lots of friends. It would make sense then that
when he wasn't around those friends, he'd want to stay in touch
with them as much as possible. They started a group chat on
their phones to be in contact regularly.

His parents supported that decision. Tyler had a good set
of friends, and his parents encouraged those friendships. But
then some drama started on the group chat, as it often does.
Some of the teenagers were getting their feelings hurt. Some
parents stepped in to help solve the communication issues and
smooth the ruffled feathers. Boundaries were given to keep
things healthier moving forward. Tyler wasn't allowed on his
phone after 9:00 p.m.

But his friends were in the middle of a big conversation. It
was summer, they weren't going to get to see one another for a
while, and he really wanted to know what was going on. It was
10:30 p.m. His parents were getting ready for bed. He knew he
was disobeying, but what would it hurt to take a quick look?

The problem was that Tyler had recently broken trust with
his parents about another issue. They were working to rebuild

trust. But that little decision to take a quick look broke more trust with his parents. They'd already given grace over some other issues. And that small choice to take a quick peek cost him his phone for a whole week and his parents' trust for a long while. Tyler thought for sure that no one would know, but the truth has a way of coming to the surface.

But even if no one else found out, God knows what's in a person's heart and mind. Second Chronicles 16:9 (NLT) says, "The eyes of the LORD search the whole earth in order to strengthen those whose hearts are fully committed to him."

God sees when you are faithful in the small things (Luke 16:10 tells us this too!)—the things you do and say and watch when no one else is looking. He doesn't do this to catch you in sin and cover you with guilt and shame. No, he is watching because He loves you and wants what is best for you. He is your constant guide, your loving Father, and your faithful friend.

Lord God, I'm so thankful that You are with me always. I'm glad to know that I'm never alone and that You are near to speak to me and help me in all my decisions, big and small.

ALL THE WRINKLES

*"If you [really] love Me, you will keep
and obey My commandments."*
JOHN 14:15 AMP

Jade was a busy girl. She had a part-time job, she played sports, she was active in youth group, and of course she had plenty of school and homework to add in there too. Every week, her mom did her laundry, but it was Jade's job to fold it and put it away.

One week was just too busy. She took her laundry basket upstairs like usual, but instead of obeying her mom to fold it right away and put it in her drawers, she left it squished in the basket to deal with another day. A few days later, she looked at her clothes and remembered she needed to put them away. She stuffed them in the drawers before heading out to youth group.

The next day as she got ready for school, she realized that every shirt she owned was a wrinkled mess in her drawer. There was no time to iron or put anything in the dryer to get out the wrinkles. Her mom worked, so she didn't have time to redo the laundry either. Jade was forced to wear wrinkles to school. On the way, she tried her best to smooth them out, but there wasn't much she could do. She was a little embarrassed, but nothing could be done. These were the natural consequences of not obeying her mom.

Jesus said that if we love Him, we will obey Him. Let's take a look at this verse in context: "If you [really] love Me, you will keep and obey My commandments. And I will ask the Father, and He will give you another Helper (Comforter, Advocate, Intercessor—Counselor, Strengthener, Standby), to be with you forever—the Spirit of Truth, whom the world cannot receive [and take to its heart] because it does not see Him or know Him, but you know Him because He (the Holy Spirit) remains with you continually and will be in you" (John 14:15–17 AMP).

Jesus wants us to obey Him because we love Him. But He doesn't just tell us to obey and leave us in our humanness—knowing we're going to run out of time. Knowing that we make lots of mistakes. Knowing that we'll get lots of wrinkles. He actually sent His very own Spirit to help us obey Him!

Yes, when we don't obey, there are often natural consequences like going to school in wrinkles. Or getting a speeding ticket when you drive too fast because you're late for work. But God's Spirit is alive in you, comforting you and teaching you how to do better next time.

Lord, I want to obey You because I love You!
Thank You for sending me a Helper.
You are awesome, God!

TAKING EVERY THOUGHT CAPTIVE

*We demolish arguments and every pretension that sets
itself up against the knowledge of God, and we take
captive every thought to make it obedient to Christ.*
2 Corinthians 10:5 niv

Want to know a secret to living a no-regrets life? Take every thought captive and make it obedient to Christ! You may be thinking, *What in the world does that mean, and how could I possibly do that?* It takes a little training and repetition, but it goes something like this: you have a thought, idea, or plan, and then you train yourself (with the help and power of the Holy Spirit) to pause and take that thought to Jesus before you do anything about it. This is important for many reasons.

Sometimes your thoughts might not be coming from God at all but from the enemy of your soul—in which case you would be believing a lie if you agree with it. Or you may have an idea that's a really good one but God wants to prepare you for it or point you in another direction before you go opening doors that aren't ready to be opened. Taking every thought captive and making it obedient to God's truth will protect you from acting on thoughts that don't align with God's will for your life.

Let's try this now. What are you thinking? Maybe you're almost late for volleyball practice and you have to run. Maybe you have a to-do list that you are ready to get started on. Pause.

Just pause for a few seconds. Now take those thoughts, ideas, and plans to Jesus.

Jesus, are these thoughts true? Are these ideas worth pursuing? Do these plans align with Your purpose for my life? Picture yourself lifting these thoughts up to Jesus as you pray. Be silent for a few moments and listen for His voice. As you grow in Christ, you will get better and better at discerning His voice.

God is the Creator of all. Creativity came from Him. He can speak to His children in whatever capacity He chooses. Are you listening? It might be a scripture that comes to mind by the power of the Holy Spirit. You might hear His beautiful creation chirping through your window. He might plant a song in your heart and a melody on your lips. He might paint a picture in your imagination as you pray.

Get used to pausing and listening. Sounds simple, but that is the pathway to living a life with no regrets. We're going to unpack this scripture a little more tomorrow.

Jesus, I want to discern Your voice in my life.
I believe that I can hear from You, and I pray
that You would help me to take every thought
captive and make it obedient to You.

DON'T BELIEVE THOSE LIES

Have you ever looked in the mirror and thought: *I wish I looked more like (fill in the blank)*, or *I wish I didn't have so many freckles? My nose is too big. My eyes are dull. My hair is ugly.* I guarantee those thoughts didn't come from God. He made you just the way you are for a purpose. He delights in you! So when you have rogue thoughts like that, you have to make them obedient to Christ and what He says is true about you.

Making your thoughts obey Christ means that you make your thoughts agree with what God says about you. You believe the truth from God's Word, and you don't believe or agree with any lies of the enemy, including any lies from other people. If you are struggling with a thought that is really getting you down, it could be a lie you're believing about yourself.

A good habit to get into is to make a list. On the left, write down any lies you might be believing. Maybe it's something about the way you look or feel. Many teenagers struggle with believing that they are ugly. The enemy really loves to use this lie against young women. Write it down and ask Jesus to reveal His truth. On the right side of the page, go through your Bible and find out what God says is true.

Here are a few truths to note:

* "I praise you because I am fearfully and wonderfully made; your works are wonderful, I know that full well" (Psalm 139:14 NIV).

* "For we are God's masterpiece. He has created us anew in Christ Jesus, so we can do the good things he planned for us long ago" (Ephesians 2:10 NLT).

* "And yet, O LORD, you are our Father. We are the clay, and you are the potter. We all are formed by your hand" (Isaiah 64:8 NLT).

These are the things God says about you. Read them. Write them down. Memorize them. Repeat them. Believe them! If anyone says otherwise, the Holy Spirit will remind you of these truths that He has written on your heart. Keep your lies-and-truths list handy so that you can remind yourself of God's truth often.

Psalm 119:133 (AMP) says, "Establish my footsteps in [the way of] Your word; do not let any human weakness have power over me [causing me to be separated from You]." Let this be your prayer today.

Lord, I repent of believing lies about myself and my worth. I will trust what Your Word says about me. You made me wonderful. I'm Your masterpiece. I was formed by Your hand.

GOOD IDEAS AND FISHING

Commit everything you do to the Lord.
Trust him, and he will help you.
PSALM 37:5 NLT

Kristen believed in God. She didn't know Him very well, but she went to church. She was in the habit of planning life herself and doing whatever she thought was best and then asking God to bless everything she decided to do. She didn't know of any other way.

But is there a better way? One pastor used a metaphor about going fishing. A boy asked his dad if he could go fishing. The dad gave his permission, and off he went. Another boy asked his dad to go fishing with him. He received not only his permission but also his blessing and his presence.

See the difference? We can ask God to bless all of our plans as part of a quick prayer on our way out the door. Or we can seek God's will, His blessing, and His presence as we have ideas and make decisions.

Sometimes we get ideas and go barreling ahead without even asking God if it's good for us or part of His plan. As believers, we have grace and freedom to make all kinds of choices. We can go off and go fishing by ourselves if we want to. But if we want to go deeper in our relationship with Jesus, we can go after His presence and His heart.

Matthew 6:31–33 (NIV) says, "So do not worry, saying, 'What shall we eat?' or 'What shall we drink?' or 'What shall we wear?'"

For the pagans run after all these things, and your heavenly Father knows that you need them. But seek first his kingdom and his righteousness, and all these things will be given to you as well."

Seeking God's kingdom first is a really good idea because God knows everything you need. He knows that you need food and clothes. No need to obsess over that. Those trivial things can be really distracting. God knows how He created you and the desires and gifts He put in your heart. You can trust Him to care for your heart well.

Jeremiah 10:12 (AMP) says, "God made the earth by His power; He established the world by His wisdom and by His understanding and skill He has stretched out the heavens."

This is the God who loves and cares about you. He is the source of all ideas and wisdom. When you seek Him and His kingdom above all else, you will find blessing in His presence.

So, what's your idea for the day? Maybe it's a great day to go fishing with Jesus!

Lord, please help me to bring my plans and ideas to You first, before I go charging through my day. I want Your presence and Your blessing in my life.

A CHANGE IN PLANS

Commit your works to the Lord [submit and trust them to Him], and your plans will succeed [if you respond to His will and guidance].
PROVERBS 16:3 AMP

Sometimes God changes plans for your good and for your protection. My kids were really disappointed that something they were looking forward to for months got canceled at the last minute. We reminded them that God knows the end from the beginning and that He sees what we can't. Perhaps some of the people involved would have been in great danger had they proceeded with the event as planned. Or maybe God had something better planned and He wanted to do some heart work, teaching them to trust and rely on Him fully.

Julie was late for an overnight trip with her friend. She packed her bags in a hurry and rushed out the door. She was frustrated with herself for being so late. It was winter, and she came to an icy spot in the road. Her car spun all the way around and ended up on the opposite side of the road. If she had been on time, she would have arrived at that same spot during higher traffic and could have been in a bad accident.

One time I was driving with my children, just about to get on the interstate, when I was prompted to go a different direction and see my husband instead. He was working close to where we happened to be, and I thought we'd stop by to say hi. As I pulled into the parking space, my car collapsed on the front right side. Somehow the bolts had come loose and the wheel came off. That was scary! It could have happened on the interstate where the speed limit was 75 mph. Instead, it happened right as the car stopped in the parking lot. We were safe. We were so thankful for that change in plans!

Sometimes God rearranges our plans like that to keep us safe. Check out these three verses:

* "We can make our plans, but the LORD determines our steps" (Proverbs 16:9 NLT).

* "You can make many plans, but the LORD's purpose will prevail" (Proverbs 19:21 NLT).

* "I know that you can do all things; no purpose of yours can be thwarted" (Job 42:2 NIV).

The Bible tells us that we can make plans, but God is in control. He determines what happens. His purpose is never thwarted. So instead of being disappointed and angry the next time your plans go awry, trust Your loving heavenly Father instead. He knows best. And He is good.

Lord, I'm sorry for having a bad attitude when things don't go my way. Please help me to see things differently. Remind me that You are in control and that You always have my best interests in mind.

KEEP ON ASKING

"Keep on asking, and you will receive what you ask for. Keep on seeking, and you will find. Keep on knocking, and the door will be opened to you. For everyone who asks, receives. Everyone who seeks, finds. And to everyone who knocks, the door will be opened."
MATTHEW 7:7–8 NLT

Kenna had a weird experience at her first job. She heard about a local pet shelter and boarding facility that hired younger teenagers, and she was excited about making her own money. She also loved taking care of pets, so she thought it was a win-win. She met the owner, and her start date was set. Although the work was a little bit stinky sometimes, she mostly enjoyed it. A few weeks went by, however, and she hadn't received her first paycheck yet. She asked about it, and the owner said she was working on it. Another week went by and then another. Kenna kept asking about her paycheck, and the owner always had an excuse for not paying. Encouraged by her mother not to work another day without getting paid, Kenna asked again about her paycheck. Finally, the owner got out her checkbook and wrote Kenna a check. She had over six weeks of payment due that she finally received. Kenna realized she didn't want to work for a boss who didn't keep her word, so she found another job.

I'm reminded of a story in the Bible that starts like this: "Then Jesus told his disciples a parable to show them that they should always pray and not give up" (Luke 18:1 NIV). Jesus went on to tell of a widow who kept going to a judge, pleading to him for justice against her adversary. The judge kept refusing, but the widow kept asking. Finally, he gave her what she wanted simply so she would stop bothering him. The point is that if an ungodly and careless judge would act on a persistent request, how much more would our God who loves us dearly act on our behalf? So don't give up on praying. Keep asking!

Jesus said similar things in Matthew 7. Keep on asking! Keep going to Jesus. And when you do, you'll find that the door is open to you. Jesus hears your prayers, and He responds.

Do you have an issue or a relationship that has been on your prayer list for a long time? Don't cross it off. Don't give up. God is listening. Are you?

Praying is not just sending your wish list up to heaven. Are you in the habit of doing a whole lot of talking to the ceiling with an "Amen" at the end? Then your prayer life might need a little transformation. More on that in our next devotion.

Lord, I'm so thankful that You hear my prayers. I'm going to keep on praying because I trust that You are good.

THE PRAYER TRANSFORMATION

The world is full of so-called prayer warriors who are prayer-ignorant. They're full of formulas and programs and advice, peddling techniques for getting what you want from God. Don't fall for that nonsense. This is your Father you are dealing with, and he knows better than you what you need. With a God like this loving you, you can pray very simply.
MATTHEW 6:7–8 MSG

There are no formulas or boxes to check when you talk to God. He is your loving Father, and He knows exactly what's on your heart. You can simply talk to Him like you would a beloved friend.

Remember, though, prayer is not just sending a wish list to heaven with lots of talking and no listening. If you're looking to transform your prayer life, here are some ideas:

* Get a journal. Start writing down your prayers and the ways God is answering them.

* Open your Bible to the Psalms and use them as prayers to God.

* Go out into God's creation and listen to all the amazing creatures He made. Thank Him for His awesome creativity and power. He is the source of life! Experience God by using all of your senses: smell the fresh air, see the beautiful

design in nature, touch the trees and grass. Psalm 34:8 (NLT) says, "Taste and see that the LORD is good. Oh, the joys of those who take refuge in him!" What can you taste in nature? A ripe blueberry? The taste of a raindrop on your tongue? God is speaking life to you!

* Be silent! Silence may seem boring, but please remember that God is the Creator of all. He can speak to His children however He chooses. As you wait patiently, expectantly, and silently in God's presence, God may surprise you with how He begins speaking! Scriptures and songs may pop into your head. He may impress His truth on your heart in some way. A special memory of being loved might come to mind. Let God speak to your heart and mind as you wait, expecting Him to be there. Check out what the Bible has to say about this:

  - "Be still, and know that I am God" (Psalm 46:10 NIV).
  - "For God alone my soul waits in silence and quietly submits to Him, for my hope is from Him" (Psalm 62:5 AMP).
  - "In the morning, LORD, you hear my voice; in the morning I lay my requests before you and wait expectantly" (Psalm 5:3 NIV).

Lord, please transform my prayer life. I want to hear from You as I pray.

BOUNDARIES AND NO REGRETS

The God who made the world and everything in it is the Lord of heaven and earth and does not live in temples built by human hands. And he is not served by human hands, as if he needed anything. Rather, he himself gives everyone life and breath and everything else. From one man he made all the nations, that they should inhabit the whole earth; and he marked out their appointed times in history and the boundaries of their lands. God did this so that they would seek him and perhaps reach out for him and find him, though he is not far from any one of us.

Acts 17:24–27 NIV

My son was reading a book recently that talked about boundaries. What if basketball had no boundaries or rules? I asked my daughter that on the way to volleyball practice. What if you were able to punch the lights out of the girl next to you to get the ball? That would be terrible, and no sensible kid would participate in something like that. You want boundaries in organized sports. Good coaches and referees help keep those boundaries in place.

Boundaries help keep you safe, and they also provide freedom. Once you know the rules, you can get better and better at the game and have freedom to give it your all. God gives us good boundaries in life, and He wants us to have healthy boundaries as we live it.

He has put you right where you are in this time and this space for a reason. You have the address you have because that's where He has placed you. He has given you boundaries and freedom within those boundaries.

Check out these verses:

* "For the grace of God has been revealed, bringing salvation to all people. And we are instructed to turn from godless living and sinful pleasures. We should live in this evil world with wisdom, righteousness, and devotion to God, while we look forward with hope to that wonderful day when the glory of our great God and Savior, Jesus Christ, will be revealed" (Titus 2:11–13 NLT).

* "Now the Lord is the Spirit, and where the Spirit of the Lord is, there is freedom" (2 Corinthians 3:17 NIV).

* "You, my brothers and sisters, were called to be free. But do not use your freedom to indulge the flesh; rather, serve one another humbly in love" (Galatians 5:13 NIV).

Freedom and healthy boundaries seem to go together well. God says to use our freedom wisely, to serve one another in love. Sounds like a no-regrets kind of life to me!

Lord, I'm thankful that You have a plan and purpose for my life that includes me being right where You put me. Thank You for the freedom You've given me! Help me to use that freedom wisely.

A SNEAKY AND GENTLE BANDIT

Trust GOD from the bottom of your heart; don't try to figure out everything on your own. Listen for GOD's voice in everything you do, everywhere you go; he's the one who will keep you on track.
PROVERBS 3:5–6 MSG

Every year around Mother's Day, we buy lots of flowers to plant in containers around our house. Ferns for the porch, impatiens for the shady areas, and geraniums and petunias for the back patio. There are certain containers that get a lot of sun and, therefore, need extra watering because they dry out quickly. I bought a new kind of potting soil to help hold moisture. Boy did I regret that this year!

A few days after I planted all my flowers and had them looking lovely, I noticed something strange. Two of my plants were dug up. The flowers I planted were lying gently on the ground next to the pot. I thought maybe the wind had blown super hard and knocked them out of their pots before they had a chance to root. I replanted them and didn't think much more about it.

But then the next day, four of my plants were dug up! One in the front of the house, two pots on the side by the garage, and one pot on the back patio. And all the pretty flowers were laid gently next to the pots. Okay. Who was playing a trick on me? My kids and husband said they didn't touch them. Our dogs wouldn't have done it so gently, so it couldn't have been their fault. I started to get a little creeped out. It almost looked like someone had come searching for a hidden key to break into our house or something! I ordered an outdoor video camera with the hope that I could catch the culprit in the act.

While I was waiting for our security camera to arrive, I had a thought. Could an animal be doing this, other than our dogs? I researched and found that raccoons are regularly known to eat certain potting soil because it contains a "fish emulsion" that they think is yummy. I checked my potting soil, and sure enough! Mystery solved.

Thankfully, our little raccoon bandit was polite and gentle, laying aside my flowers as he did. I found some raccoon deterrent, and he left my pots alone after that.

Sometimes in life you walk right into something you'll regret without even knowing it, like my choice to buy that potting soil. Today's verse is about trusting God when you don't understand what's going on. When you're baffled by something, take it to Jesus and listen for His voice. He'll help you figure it out.

Thank You, Lord, for leading me when I don't know what to do. I trust You, Jesus!

WISDOM: ON- AND OFF-ROAD

Get all the advice and instruction you can,
so you will be wise the rest of your life.
PROVERBS 19:20 NLT

Jake started taking driver's ed after he turned sixteen. At the end of several of the classes, the instructor shared videos of true stories that illustrated how teens had made unwise choices while driving that had caused problems, some of which were deadly.

Some videos showed the effects of drinking and driving, and others showed the effects of texting while driving. All of those videos showed a lack of wisdom on the driver's part. One video was particularly startling. It showed a beautiful teenage girl who had been hit by a young distracted driver. Her car caught on fire from the crash, and her body was severely burned all over. Later on, she went on national TV to tell her story and help prevent other young drivers from causing similar accidents and heartbreak. Her face was, and still is, unrecognizable.

A quick decision to look down at your phone while driving can cause extreme consequences that you may regret for the rest of your life. It takes a lot of wisdom to prevent and avoid distraction while you're driving. Teens who are addicted to drugs, alcohol, or screens can make dangerous decisions on the road.

Make a commitment right now to stay away from anything that could impair your driving ability. If you know that you spend too much time on your phone or other screens, ask your parents or a trusted adult for help. If you're used to having your phone in your hands at all times, it will be hard to put it down when you get in the car.

The Bible talks a lot about wisdom, and that's exactly what you need in a situation like this. Take a look at these scriptures about wisdom:

* "If you need wisdom, ask our generous God, and he will give it to you. He will not rebuke you for asking" (James 1:5 NLT).

* "So be careful how you live. Don't live like fools, but like those who are wise. Make the most of every opportunity in these evil days. Don't act thoughtlessly, but understand what the Lord wants you to do" (Ephesians 5:15–17 NLT).

* "For the LORD gives wisdom; from his mouth come knowledge and understanding" (Proverbs 2:6 NIV).

* "How much better to get wisdom than gold, to get insight rather than silver!" (Proverbs 16:16 NIV).

These verses are great to memorize when you start driving. But, of course, they're useful for anyone at any time and any age. The Bible praises finding wisdom more than finding gold. Wisdom's value far exceeds that of riches.

Lord, as I begin driving — and always — help me to come to You as the source of all wisdom.

MIRACLES AND DOUBTS

Be on guard. Stand firm in the faith.
Be courageous. Be strong.
1 Corinthians 16:13 NLT

In the Old Testament, God brought the Israelites out of Egypt and they existed in a desert land where there was no water for forty years. These people were eyewitnesses of God's miraculous power when He split the sea for them to walk through. They ran out of food and had no water, so God sent them manna from heaven—a miraculous food that they had never seen or heard of before. He provided water for them out of a rock. They had all the evidence they needed that God was with them. He saw them. He was caring for their needs. But what did these people do when Moses took too long up on the mountain? They began "deconstructing." They forgot what God had done. Or maybe they remembered but just didn't care anymore because they were sick of camping out in the desert for so long. (Can you imagine camping for forty years? No thank you!)

Deconstructing isn't a new thing. It's happened since ancient times. When faith is tested, some people just decide they don't believe God is real anymore, and they choose to leave the narrow path. If doubts start creeping into your heart and mind, here are some things you can do:

Write down the miracles! You can find miracles all through the Bible to point to. You can also point to times when God has done the miraculous in your own life. Take some time and write out the prayer requests that God has answered. Date them. Write about how you felt about His answers. Write down the circumstances behind the story so that you can go back when you're having doubts and see how God came through for you at just the right time. When something miraculous and amazing happens in your life, you think at the time that you'll never forget. But just look at the Israelites! They forgot or ignored what God had done and decided to worship other idols instead of the one and only God of the universe. So record His great works in your life, friend. Write down what God says and does. At our home, we have written about miracles in our journals but also on a giant sticky note that covers part of a wall. We can look at that and remember that God is real and is actively working in our lives.

Another thing to do is to surround yourself with people who are choosing to love Jesus and His Word. God wants us to encourage each other in our faith.

Lord, when I'm tempted to doubt Your love or existence, remind me of all the amazing miracles You've done in my life!

DON'T MISS THE FOREST

Jesus replied: " 'Love the Lord your God with all your heart and with all your soul and with all your mind.' This is the first and greatest commandment. And the second is like it: 'Love your neighbor as yourself.' "
Matthew 22:37–39 NIV

This past spring, I was looking for two specific trees for my yard. I went to the local landscape nursery and drove up the long lane to the greenhouse. I had no trouble at all finding a young apple tree inside. But the folks who owned the place were busy when I was looking for the evergreen, so I didn't get a chance to ask for help. I saw a few spindly and small evergreens, but not what I was looking for at all. I drove home a little confused that this large landscape nursery didn't have what I was looking for.

A few weeks later I was driving to another part of town. I drove straight past the landscape nursery. I noticed the long lane I had driven up to the greenhouse. And guess what was planted on both sides of the lane: Evergreens! Row after row of trees and evergreens for sale. I had literally missed the forest for the trees. It never occurred to me that the long lane of trees I was driving past were for sale. Talk about a "duh" moment!

Living a "no-regrets life" means that you don't get so caught up in the details that you miss the big picture of life. High school and sports and hobbies and boys can begin to consume too much of your time and attention if you're not focused on the big picture. You don't want to graduate and look back on the last four years of your life and realize you missed the point.

What is your big picture? What do you want your life to be about? It's time to decide and live your life on mission.

God's "big picture mission" for each of us is clear: love Him and love others as you love yourself. As Christians, we follow Jesus' directive to go into all the world and live out that mission (Matthew 28:18–20). How we do that looks different for each believer.

So take a minute to take stock of your life: Do the sports and hobbies you are pursuing line up with that mission? Can you share the love of Jesus while you're doing them? What about your relationships? Does this boy you think is cute join you in your mission to love and follow Jesus?

Remember: don't miss the forest for the trees. If you get distracted by all the little details, it's easy to lose sight of the big picture God has for you.

Lord, please show me how I can share Your love with others as I pursue the things that matter most.

LITTLE DISTRACTIONS

I will meditate on your precepts and
fix my eyes on your ways.
PSALM 119:15 ESV

Little distractions can turn into big regrets pretty quickly. We talked about how that can happen dangerously when you're driving. But it can happen in everyday life too.

Maybe you're writing a paper and your phone keeps going off with all kinds of notifications, but you can't shut it off because you're not at home and your mom needs to be able to reach you, so silencing those dings won't work. You get the idea. Sometimes distraction management gets complicated. But if you don't finish that paper, you'll be in trouble at school. What can you do?

Or consider this: have you ever had two or more really big events coming up at the same time? It can be super hard to stay focused on the one while ideas for the others keep popping into your head. This happened to Kami. She realized a little too late that she had signed up and committed to too many things at once. She didn't find out until later that everything would culminate during the same week. She was distracted by all the little details and was dropping balls all over the place. Instead of doing really well in one of her best events, she was mediocre in everything and extremely disappointed in herself. Everything had sounded so fun at first. She knew she could do well at everything she signed up for, but it was just too much at once, and she was overly distracted.

Is there an answer? Yes! Take those thoughts captive! That can be a prayer that looks something like this: *Jesus, what is my focus supposed to be here? What should I say yes to? Please help me to stay on track.*

Then pause to listen as Jesus guides you. Overcommitment leads to being overly distracted. Saying no can be difficult when you are growing up. Especially when things look fun and you'd love doing them. And sometimes you say yes too many times simply because you don't like to disappoint people. Do you struggle with either of those issues?

If so, talk to Jesus about this. He knows why you do the things you do. And He loves and delights in you. He wants you to come to Him about every decision so that He can help you through it. You'll be amazed to see how Jesus leads you in the right direction every time you take your choices to Him. He really does see. He really does care. And He wants the very best for you.

Jesus, my life seems so full of choices.
Would You help me to make wise ones?
Help me to stay focused when all of life's
little distractions come dinging! Help
me to fix my eyes on Your ways.

WHAT IS TRUTH?

Do not quench [subdue, or be unresponsive to the working and guidance of] the [Holy] Spirit. Do not scorn or reject gifts of prophecy or prophecies [spoken revelations— words of instruction or exhortation or warning]. But test all things carefully [so you can recognize what is good]. Hold firmly to that which is good. Abstain from every form of evil [withdraw and keep away from it].

1 THESSALONIANS 5:19–22 AMP

My kids were invited to go to a youth group at another church. They both wanted to go because so many of their friends go there. We allowed them to visit, and they both loved it. So we talked with the youth pastor, and he was happy to have them come. He shared his vision for his youth group, and we share similar values and love for God. We decided to allow them to go to this youth group regularly, even though that's not where we attend church on Sundays.

We know many of the other teens in the youth group, but we don't know any of the other leaders there at all yet. The teens split into small groups and have discussions with these leaders. We have talks with Jake and Jessa on the way home from youth group about what they discussed and what they're learning.

But we've been very clear with our kids that just because someone leads at a church doesn't mean they get it right all the time. We've been training our kids to go to the source of wisdom: God Himself. Anything they hear about God, even if it's from someone they trust, they are to compare with God's Word to find out if it lines up.

Remember what Jesus said in John 14:26? Here it is again: "But the Helper (Comforter, Advocate, Intercessor—Counselor, Strengthener, Standby), the Holy Spirit, whom the Father will send in My name [in My place, to represent Me and act on My behalf], He will teach you all things. And He will help you remember everything that I have told you" (AMP).

Jesus said that His Spirit will teach you and remind you of all the things that Jesus said. His Spirit is alive inside you, leading you and guiding you in the truth. If you hear something strange about God and get a little nudge in your heart, pay attention to that warning signal. It's often God's Spirit directing you to find out what His Word really says about the matter. John 16:13 (NIV) says, "But when he, the Spirit of truth, comes, he will guide you into all the truth."

Lord, I know You're the source of all wisdom and truth. Help me to be sensitive to Your leading in my life. Show me the truth when I get those little nudges from You.

HERE WE GO AGAIN, PART 1

*I don't really understand myself, for I want to do what
is right, but I don't do it. Instead, I do what I hate.*

Romans 7:15 NLT

Uh-oh. Katie knew she was in big trouble. She made a contract with her parents because she had a hard time sticking to her screen-time limits. She knew it was a problem, and she wanted help. So she committed to the following: not touching her phone until after 9:00 a.m., enjoying two hours of free phone usage (permission could be given for extra time if she asked), and making sure her phone was put away on the kitchen dock by 9:00 p.m. She also agreed that consequences would be the loss of her phone for one week if she went outside those boundaries.

She did well with this contract for a while. She was even getting pretty proud of herself for having some self-control. But then she got up early one morning with extra time on her hands. Her mom wasn't even awake. Her phone was just staring at her in the kitchen. What could a quick look hurt? You can guess what happened next.

Her mom discovered that Katie had used her phone outside of the contract boundaries, and Katie received the consequences she had agreed to. Katie was extremely disappointed in herself. She went to her mom and asked sadly, "Why do I do this?"

Katie's mom got out her Bible and showed her the apostle Paul's struggle with sin in Romans 7. He knew the right thing to do but had trouble always doing it. It's the human condition.

Have you ever struggled over and over with doing something you knew you shouldn't do?

So what is the answer?

Check this out: "Oh, what a miserable person I am! Who will free me from this life that is dominated by sin and death? Thank God! The answer is in Jesus Christ our Lord" (Romans 7:24–25 NLT).

But what does that mean, and how does it help?

If you struggle in this area, I encourage you to get on the Bible App or go online to Biblegateway.com and look up Romans 7 and 8 in *The Message* paraphrase.

Tomorrow we'll see how Katie's situation played out, but for today, get your journal and give yourself some space and time with Jesus. Read Romans 7 and 8 and ask God what He wants you to learn from all of this. If you've committed your life to Jesus, His Spirit is alive and working in you. You can hear from Him directly. So go to Him now.

Jesus, I messed up again. I'm sorry. I was trying to do things in my own strength, and I failed. Cover me again with Your grace and mercy. Help me to know that You still love me. I want to hear from You.

HERE WE GO AGAIN, PART 2

With the arrival of Jesus, the Messiah, that fateful dilemma is resolved. Those who enter into Christ's being-here-for-us no longer have to live under a continuous, low-lying black cloud. A new power is in operation. The Spirit of life in Christ, like a strong wind, has magnificently cleared the air, freeing you from a fated lifetime of brutal tyranny at the hands of sin and death. . . . Those who trust God's action in them find that God's Spirit is in them—living and breathing God!
ROMANS 8:1–2, 6 MSG

As Katie and her parents prayed, God gave them wisdom in new ways. Katie was really struggling with screen addiction, and so they realized that this wouldn't be an easy fix. If Katie had a health issue like diabetes or needed to lose weight, they wouldn't leave cupcakes and candy on the kitchen counter for her to pass by countless times a day just so she could build up her willpower. That would be cruel. But how could they apply that kind of thinking to screen addiction?

Katie's parents wanted to support her as she learned to walk with Jesus in this area. They came up with a plan where, after hours, Katie would put her phone in a place that she couldn't get to without her parents knowing. This was a relief to Katie and took away the temptation to sneak. Katie knew she was powerless in and of herself to control her phone addiction.

Have you ever heard of a 12-step program? It's used in

addiction recovery all over the world, and it can apply to most addictions. Even screen addictions.

The very first step is to admit you are powerless to change on your own. The second step is to believe that a higher power can help. And the third is to let Him have control.

Here's the deal: As a follower of Jesus, you have the Spirit of the living God at work in you. The power to overcome is from Him alone, not from anything you can do. If you submit to His rule in your heart, He will give you fresh strength, energy, and ideas to walk in freedom with Him.

The fourth step? That's to take a personal inventory of what's going on inside that led to the addiction in the first place. It might take awhile for Katie to have complete freedom over her screen time. She has some healing that needs to take place in her heart first.

And that's God's specialty.

Lord God, I know I am in Your all-powerful hands. I release control over myself and my struggle to You. Open up my heart and look inside. Show me my sin. Heal what needs healing. Correct what needs correcting. I choose to follow You and walk with You in this.

SELF-CONFIDENCE OR GOD-CONFIDENCE?

Therefore let the one who thinks he stands firm [immune to temptation, being overconfident and self-righteous], take care that he does not fall [into sin and condemnation].

1 CORINTHIANS 10:12 AMP

Remember how Katie was getting pretty proud of herself for having some self-control? That's a red flag. Want to know why? Because she started relying on her own power and strength instead of on God's.

The Message says it this way: "Forget about self-confidence; it's useless. Cultivate God-confidence."

People do that a lot, you know. Even Christians. They rely on self-confidence. They trust their own power and self-control. Some theologians call that "temporary atheism." In other words, a person believes in God but then forgets about Him in their day-to-day choices. Then they add Him back in whenever they feel like it. Like maybe on Sundays.

It's a common thing to do a good job at something for a while, then get overconfident and proud, and then mess up. That's what today's verse is all about. Here's an example: I was playing the keyboard for a worship service once. I took a look at the production sheet before rehearsal, saw what song they wanted me to play, realized that I'd played that song many, many times, and thought I didn't need to practice. I didn't even open up the file to see the chord chart or listen to the song arrangement. But when I got to the rehearsal, I soon found out that they were playing a new arrangement of the song, and I didn't know it at all. I was overconfident, and I messed up. Talk about embarrassing!

Does all this growing-up business have you stressed? You are not alone. And you don't have to go through anything alone. The very next verse has something important to say too: "The temptations in your life are no different from what others experience. And God is faithful. He will not allow the temptation to be more than you can stand. When you are tempted, he will show you a way out so that you can endure" (1 Corinthians 10:13 NLT).

The stuff you're struggling with might make you feel isolated. Don't listen to those lies of the enemy. Other people have been through this. And God is with you. His power is alive and at work in you.

Instead of being full of self-confidence and believing that you're immune to temptation, humbly walk with Jesus day by day, relying on Him for wisdom and strength to do what He is calling you to do.

Lord, I'm thankful that I'm not alone and that You've provided a way out when I'm tempted to do something I know I shouldn't do. Help me to rely on You day by day.

TEMPTATION TO SIN

Each person is tempted when they are dragged
away by their own evil desire and enticed.
Then, after desire has conceived, it gives birth to sin;
and sin, when it is full-grown, gives birth to death.
Don't be deceived, my dear brothers and sisters.

JAMES 1:14–16 NIV

A man was fired from his job because he kept missing meetings. The big problem with that was that he was one of the managers! He was required to be there. So, some of his staff would walk by his desk, and there he was—glued to his screen. He missed so many meetings and project deadlines that some of his staff finally went over his head and complained to the manager's boss. He was fired. When the tech team went to clean out his desk and dismantle the computer, they found the strangest things. This man had sticky notes with lists of produce like tomatoes and corn and pumpkins. Then they found evidence on his computer that he had been playing a computer game about farming. He had become addicted, and it cost him his job. True story!

Of all the games you could play, a farming game seems so innocent and nice, right? But just like any distraction, you can easily get sucked in, and before you know it, hours have passed. That's what happened to this manager. He didn't mean for it to happen. He is certainly regretting his decision now.

It's the enemy's way to distract you from real life. Something that you think would never trip you up suddenly has.

I was distracted recently. I was working on a project with a deadline. I knew I needed to focus. Someone texted me a note of encouragement after they read something I wrote. It said, "You are amazing!" I was suddenly tempted to go back and read whatever it was that they thought was amazing. I might like to agree with them about myself, right? Maybe I'd like to feel good about that and puff myself up a little. But I quickly realized the truth for what it was. The intent of my friend was good. But this could quickly turn into a distraction from the enemy. If I took my focus off my project and went down the rabbit trail of pride, I could miss my deadline. I had to stay focused! So, what can we do before those little temptations that come at us become big and unmanageable?

Take those thoughts captive and make them obedient to Christ (2 Corinthians 10:5)! In my situation, God reminded me that He is the giver of all good gifts and that He alone gets the glory. And then I carried on with my project. Crisis averted!

Lord, please plant the truth of 2 Corinthians 10:5 deep in my heart. Holy Spirit, remind me of this discipline every time I'm tempted and distracted. Let my heart and mind obey You!

TEARS AND FEARS

Don't worry about anything; instead, pray about everything.
Tell God what you need, and thank him for all he has done.
PHILIPPIANS 4:6 NLT

My daughter broke her leg when she was ten years old. It was a bad break, damaging her growth plate. She has healed up nicely over the past two years, and doctors have been monitoring the growth of her leg regularly. We went back for more x-rays recently, however, and found a concern.

The surgeon explained that one area of her leg is growing and the other isn't. If we don't fix it, her ankle will grow crooked. He determined she's going to need another surgery to repair the problem. This was not good news, and Jessa was understandably upset. We all were. Fear started to creep into our thoughts. Tears made an appearance too.

After the appointment, we gathered to pray. And just like a good and comforting Father, God had something prepared for us right after we received the news. It was no coincidence that our devotions that morning were about aligning our lives with God's truth. We had been learning about the "armor of God" in Ephesians 6, and we were at the part about putting on the belt, or girdle, of truth. It's what holds us all together and keeps everything in the right place—including our feelings.

As we were reading and praying, the Holy Spirit brought John 16:33 (NIV) to mind, which says, "I have told you these things, so that in me you may have peace. In this world you will have trouble. But take heart! I have overcome the world."

So what did we do? We kicked out fear together. We didn't want to align ourselves with lies from the enemy. We didn't want to be ruled by our feelings. And we asked for the peace of Jesus to dwell in our hearts and minds instead. That's the truth we needed to align ourselves with!

The surgery was scheduled for several months later. Imagine how much time and joy would be wasted if Jessa let fear take root in her heart for all that time. God wanted to take care of that right away in the beginning and get that fear kicked out the door.

Jesus tells us that trouble will come to us as we live life in a fallen world. But we can have peace in Him! No matter what comes our way. We don't have to be afraid because He is with us.

Here's some more truth you can count on: "I prayed to the Lord, and he answered me. He freed me from all my fears" (Psalm 34:4 NLT).

God, You are so good and loving! Thank You for letting me know how close You are. You see me. You care. Fill me with Your peace as I kick fear to the curb in Jesus' name!

I'LL BE OKAY

*We have this hope as an anchor for
the soul, firm and secure.*
HEBREWS 6:19 NIV

Surgery was a few months away for Jessa, but it was still looming in the back of her head. We kicked fear out the door together. But fear likes to come back and knock again and again to see if anyone will let him in. Jessa needed an anchor for her soul as she awaited the procedure.

The *Collins Dictionary* defines *anchor* as "any of various devices dropped by a chain, cable, or rope to the bottom of a body of water for preventing or restricting the motion of a vessel or other floating object, typically having broad, hooklike arms that bury themselves in the bottom to provide a firm hold."

The writer of Hebrews tells us that our hope in Christ is an anchor for our souls. Hebrews 6:18 (AMP) explains who this hope belongs to: "We who have fled [to Him] for refuge would have strong encouragement and indwelling strength to hold tightly to the hope set before us."

Have you fled to Jesus for refuge, encouragement, and indwelling strength? Then you have Christ as an anchor for your soul. When you hold tightly to Him, He prevents you from being tossed around by the waves. And you don't have to worry about your arms giving out. That "indwelling strength" to hold on comes from God Himself. Deuteronomy 33:27 (NIV) says, "The eternal God is your refuge, and underneath are the everlasting arms."

If Jessa's hope was in a problem-free life, she would be sadly disappointed. But since her hope is in Christ, she's going to be okay. When fear tries to sneak back in and toss her around, she can hang tightly to her anchor.

A popular song on the radio says "I'll be okay" over and over. Sometimes you have to tell that to yourself again and again. Sing it! The songwriter says her hope amid the waves is that Jesus is with her.

She'll be okay. Jessa will be okay.

What about you?

Is your anchor in self-comfort?

Is your anchor in a problem- and pain-free life?

Is your anchor in your friends and what they think of you?

If you struggle with this, talk to Jesus about what's going on in your heart. He wants to show you that you can depend on Him. You can trust that His everlasting arms will take over when yours are feeling weak.

Is your anchor in Jesus? Then you'll be okay too.

Lord, You are my anchor, my hope, and my strength. I trust that Your everlasting arms are carrying me at all times. When fear tries to toss me around, remind me that I'm safe with You. I know I'll be okay because You're always with me.

FEAR AND REGRET

*"So do not fear, for I am with you; do not be dismayed,
for I am your God. I will strengthen you and help you;
I will uphold you with my righteous right hand."*

ISAIAH 41:10 NIV

Fear can be paralyzing. There are over five hundred listed and recognized phobias. A phobia is typically a fear of something that probably won't cause you any harm. Alektorophobia is the fear of chickens. Achluophobia is the fear of darkness. Hydrophobia is the fear of water. There are weather-related phobias and insect-related phobias. Maybe you've heard of this one: arachnophobia—the fear of spiders. (That one's totally understandable, right? Ew!) There are even fears of flowers, books, and clocks!

People who struggle with these phobias are often frozen in fear that they don't understand and don't know what to do with. Here's the truth, though: fear is a liar. Fear will tell you the worst-case scenario about a situation: The chickens are going to peck out your eyeballs. There is a creepy predator in the dark. You will slip and drown in the water. . . . You get the idea!

Fear can keep you from enjoying your life. And then you look back on all the things you missed out on because of fear, and you are filled with regret.

Georgia was afraid of failure in high school. She had a great singing voice and a dynamic personality, but she had some deep fears that had taken root in her. She really wanted to try out for the musical as a lead character, but she was too afraid. Afraid that she wasn't good enough. Afraid of what others would think and say about her during the audition. So instead of enjoying that special time of being a cast member in a musical, she missed out because of her fears. And she regretted that decision for many years.

If you struggle with a fear of some kind, here's a verse to memorize: "Have I not commanded you? Be strong and courageous. Do not be frightened, and do not be dismayed, for the LORD your God is with you wherever you go" (Joshua 1:9 ESV).

The key in this verse is that "God is with you wherever you go." He is the one who gives you strength and courage. You don't have to pretend to have it.

As you seek God in each situation, bring Him all of your fears and picture yourself laying them down at His feet. He will fill you with His strength and courage instead.

Lord, I have some fears I need help letting go of. Would You show me what to do? I don't want to keep carrying these around and live a life of regret. Please take my fears away and fill me with Your strength and courage.

PEACE IN PLACE OF FEAR

"Peace I leave with you; my peace I give you. I do not give to you as the world gives. Do not let your hearts be troubled and do not be afraid."

JOHN 14:27 NIV

Recently there was a little boy who had gone through cancer treatment and was on the other side of it. He wanted to share his story to encourage our church, so the pastor invited him up front and asked him some questions. The pastor asked him what he had learned from going through all of that and his response was one I will never forget. He said he learned "not to be afraid of the things of this world, and that Jesus is always with me."

This little boy had been face-to-face with death, and Jesus became very real to Him. He learned that Jesus was the source of eternal life, and that he didn't have to be afraid of life or death. Jesus gave this boy the peace that passes understanding mentioned in Philippians 4:7 (NIV): "The peace of God, which transcends all understanding, will guard your hearts and your minds in Christ Jesus."

Remember the verse right before it? Here it is again: "Don't worry about anything; instead, pray about everything. Tell God what you need, and thank him for all he has done" (Philippians 4:6 NLT).

When you refuse to worry and, instead, take everything to Jesus in prayer, He gives you a supernatural peace that goes beyond human understanding. That's what this little boy had—supernatural peace.

The Amplified Bible says verse 7 this way: "And the peace of God [that peace which reassures the heart, that peace] which transcends all understanding, [that peace which] stands guard over your hearts and your minds in Christ Jesus [is yours]."

And *The Message* says this: "Before you know it, a sense of God's wholeness, everything coming together for good, will come and settle you down. It's wonderful what happens when Christ displaces worry at the center of your life."

Do you have some very real fears in your life? Jesus is serious when He says that you can have peace and not be troubled or afraid. He will reassure your heart as that sense of everything coming together for good settles over you.

Cancer and death are no match for Jesus. "For I am convinced that neither death nor life, neither angels nor demons, neither the present nor the future, nor any powers, neither height nor depth, nor anything else in all creation, will be able to separate us from the love of God that is in Christ Jesus our Lord" (Romans 8:38–39 NIV).

Jesus, You have conquered death, and I am asking that You conquer my fear too. I believe that You can give me supernatural peace. I trust You, Jesus.

TWO CHOICES

Don't you realize that you become the slave of whatever you choose to obey? You can be a slave to sin, which leads to death, or you can choose to obey God, which leads to righteous living. Thank God! Once you were slaves of sin, but now you wholeheartedly obey this teaching we have given you. Now you are free from your slavery to sin, and you have become slaves to righteous living.

ROMANS 6:16–18 NLT

This past Sunday, our pastor gave a message about our culture. The song he chose to introduce the sermon is about a guy who continually makes bad choices, lies, does drugs, and does whatever he wants to but says that he still talks to Jesus.

The pastor chose that song to highlight how our culture is driven by consumerism. Many people, even Christians, have a transactional view of God. People do what they want and become slaves to themselves. But then they still want to talk to Jesus and hope that He does something good for them.

He went on to say that we all have only two choices in life, and you too have to decide: Will you be a slave to yourself, or will you follow Jesus?

One way leads to sin, death, disappointment, destruction, and hell. The other leads to abundant life, a relationship with Jesus, and eternity with God in heaven. The pastor reminded us that "God is a gentleman, and if you want to go down your own path, you can go." God will let you choose that.

Deuteronomy 30:19 (NLT) says, "Today I have given you the choice between life and death, between blessings and curses. Now I call on heaven and earth to witness the choice you make. Oh, that you would choose life, so that you and your descendants might live!"

Will you choose God or yourself? Life or death? It's a daily choice. Jesus Himself said, "If any of you wants to be my follower, you must give up your own way, take up your cross daily, and follow me" (Luke 9:23 NLT).

It's hard to give up our own way, isn't it? But when we do, we begin to "reflect the glory of the Lord. And the Lord—who is the Spirit—makes us more and more like him as we are changed into his glorious image" (2 Corinthians 3:18 NLT).

Lord, I'm not very good at giving up my own way. Would You help me? I want to know what it means to follow You. I choose You! I choose life! Please make me more and more like You as You change me from the inside out.

THE GOLDEN RULE

"So in everything, do to others what you would have them do to you, for this sums up the Law and the Prophets."
Matthew 7:12 NIV

The Golden Rule is not just a Christian thing; many of the world's religions have some form of this statement: "Do to others as you would have them do to you." I'm sure you've heard this time and time again. Or even, "If you don't have anything nice to say, don't say anything at all."

But as followers of Jesus, we go a step further. We love!

Romans 12:9–10 (NLT) says, "Don't just pretend to love others. Really love them. Hate what is wrong. Hold tightly to what is good. Love each other with genuine affection, and take delight in honoring each other."

The people in the world are so at odds with one another. Yes, we hate sin and what it does to people. But we don't hate the person. We are called to love the person. This is what many Christians seem to have forgotten. And yet the Bible clearly states that our battle is not against flesh and blood (Ephesians 6:12). Our battle is against the sin and evil that people are influenced by.

And we don't just pretend to love them. People can usually smell phony love a mile away. We really love them. First Peter 4:8 (NIV) says, "Above all, love each other deeply, because love covers over a multitude of sins." What does that look like? *The Message* gives us some ideas: "Most of all, love each other as if your life depended on it. Love makes up for practically anything. Be quick to give a meal to the hungry, a bed to the homeless—cheerfully. Be generous with the different things God gave you, passing them around so all get in on it: if words, let it be God's words; if help, let it be God's hearty help. That way, God's bright presence will be evident in everything through Jesus, and he'll get all the credit as the One mighty in everything—encores to the end of time. Oh, yes!" (1 Peter 4:8–11 MSG).

What's something in this list that you could do for others today? How can you be generous with the things God has given you? How could you honor the people whom God has placed in your life?

Take some time and brainstorm with Jesus in your journal. Then make a plan and do it!

Jesus, would You please fill my heart with love for others? I know You are the source of that love. When I see angry and hurting people, give me compassion for the hurt in their hearts that is causing them to act out in harmful ways. Please give me a generous heart that honors others.

LOVE AND UNITY

And over all these virtues put on love,
which binds them all together in perfect unity.
Colossians 3:14 NIV

Stacey's dad was a pastor. Sometimes it was a great life, and sometimes church ministry life was hard. It was like her family was in a fishbowl and everyone wanted to know everything about them all the time. Privacy was difficult. Knowing how and when to express feelings and emotions was difficult. And sometimes it was hard to know who you could trust in a church family.

Psalm 133:1 (NIV) says, "How good and pleasant it is when God's people live together in unity!" The body of Christ has a lot of different denominations and beliefs. If you look up a church's website, you'll often find their "statement of faith." Many of these statements contain a phrase like this: "In essentials, unity; in nonessentials, liberty; in all things, charity."

Christians have different opinions and interpretations of scriptures sometimes because of their backgrounds, how they were raised, and even due to trauma they have experienced.

But take a look at today's verse again. Love is what binds the diversity of believers together in unity. You can have great biblical knowledge and still miss the point. First Corinthians 8:1 (NIV) says, "Knowledge puffs up while love builds up." And 1 Corinthians 13:13 (NIV) says, "And now these three remain: faith, hope and love. But the greatest of these is love."

Stacey's dad was a very learned man. He had a doctorate in

theology. But he was also remarkably loving and humble. During a conversation with someone he completely disagreed with, he simply and humbly said, "That's not my understanding, but...," and then he went on to share his heart. He didn't put down the other person for their viewpoint. He didn't argue them to the ground. Humility and love won the day!

Philippians 3:15–16 (NLT) is like that. It says, "Let all who are spiritually mature agree on these things. If you disagree on some point, I believe God will make it plain to you. But we must hold on to the progress we have already made."

If you come up against someone who believes differently than you, put your love on and speak and act with humility. Let the Holy Spirit be the Holy Spirit. Let God speak to them and "make it plain." Only He can change people's hearts and minds.

Remember, "a gentle answer turns away wrath, but a harsh word stirs up anger" (Proverbs 15:1 NIV).

Lord, I agree with Your Word in Galatians 5:6 (NIV) that says, "The only thing that counts is faith expressing itself through love." Let Your Spirit bring that to my mind when I'm talking with someone with whom I disagree.

NO-REGRETS FRIENDSHIPS

So speak encouraging words to one another.
Build up hope so you'll all be together in this,
no one left out, no one left behind. I know you're
already doing this; just keep on doing it.

1 THESSALONIANS 5:11 MSG

Jenna moved to a new town and was excited to get involved in her local church and youth group. She just turned thirteen, and she was finally old enough to go. She made some friends and went to summer camp. Some of the other girls in her cabin started doing and saying things that Jenna thought were wrong. But she really wanted to fit in. It was a hard place for her to be. After camp she hung out with the same group of girls. Little by little, she let things slide that used to cause her to cringe. Soon she was acting like the rest of them.

Jenna's parents began to notice her change in attitude. And the more they began to understand what was happening, the more they knew they needed a change for Jenna. As they prayed, God led them to a different church with a different youth group. Jenna found some mature and godly friends to hang out with. They were really good influences on her life, and she was grateful. She was having a lot more good, clean, and God-honoring fun than she was at the last place.

Did you know that the Bible has quite a bit to say about the friends you choose? Check out some of these verses:

* "Walk with the wise and become wise; associate with fools and get in trouble" (Proverbs 13:20 NLT).

* "Do not be deceived: 'Bad company corrupts good morals'" (1 Corinthians 15:33 AMP).

* "Don't befriend angry people or associate with hot-tempered people, or you will learn to be like them and endanger your soul" (Proverbs 22:24–25 NLT).

* "You use steel to sharpen steel, and one friend sharpens another" (Proverbs 27:17 MSG).

Basically, the people you choose to hang out with regularly are the ones you become like. They influence you greatly, whether you realize it or not. That's why it's so important to choose your closest friends wisely.

Jenna could have ended up a very different person with a very different future if she had kept hanging around that first group of friends. If you feel like you're stuck in some friendships that you regret, talk to Jesus about this. Ask Him to give you a way out and wisdom to change. Then talk to a godly adult in your life. Ask for help and accountability. It might not be easy to find a new group of friends, but with God's help and guidance, you can do it.

Lord, help me to pay attention when those alarm bells go off inside of me that someone isn't a safe person to trust. Please give me wisdom as I make friends.

NO-REGRETS TALK

*It is foolish to belittle one's neighbor; a sensible person
keeps quiet. A gossip goes around telling secrets, but
those who are trustworthy can keep a confidence.*
PROVERBS 11:12–13 NLT

Have you ever been part of a conversation where you said too much and then worried about it afterward? This happened to Emma. She was hanging out with a new friend, and they were having a good time. Then her friend started asking her some personal questions about another friend. Emma didn't know how to respond, and she didn't want to offend her new friend, so she answered her friend's question and immediately regretted it. Emma told more than she should have, and it turned into gossip about another person. Emma felt bad and didn't know how to fix the problem.

Gossip is a sneaky sin. You're having a good talk with a friend, and then suddenly another person you both know is brought into the conversation. If you have good and encouraging things to say about that person, great! But if you have to glance at the door to see if anyone else is around to hear what you're saying, that's a good indicator that it shouldn't be said! Or if you would be ashamed or embarrassed that the text you wrote about someone got forwarded, that's probably not a good idea either.

"I'd rather not say" is a good phrase to practice. You can say this a lot of ways: *I can't talk about that right now. I'm not comfortable talking about that. Can we talk about something else?* Find a phrase that is simple for you to say, and practice it. (Seriously, it helps to practice it out loud!) You do not have to answer every question a friend asks you. If you are feeling pressured to answer, pray and ask God for help in that moment. Ask Him for wisdom and courage to change the subject. Ask Him for a way out of the conversation if you need it.

Emma talked to God about her conversation before bed that night. She repented of gossiping with her new friend and asked God for help to know what to do in that kind of situation in the future.

The Bible has some things to say about gossip:

* "A troublemaker plants seeds of strife; gossip separates the best of friends" (Proverbs 16:28 NLT).

* "A gossip betrays a confidence; so avoid anyone who talks too much" (Proverbs 20:19 NIV).

Bottom line? Don't gossip. It destroys relationships and hurts people. Stick to encouraging words that you won't regret.

Lord, I'm sorry for gossiping. Help me pay attention to Your Spirit inside me when I get that "red-flag feeling" in a conversation. Help me learn to honor You with my words.

NO-REGRETS WORK

Work willingly at whatever you do, as though you were working for the Lord rather than for people.
COLOSSIANS 3:23 NLT

Evie's dad was a good man. He loved God and he loved his family. He served in his church and had a good job where he was employed for a long time. He worked his way up to become the manager. Evie was thankful that she had such an awesome dad.

One day, Evie's dad came home and said that he was convicted about some things. He realized that he wasn't taking God to work with him. His family didn't understand, so they sat patiently as he explained. He said that when he got to work, he often forgot about God. He did his job and stayed very focused, but he rarely prayed about anything and just did the work he knew he needed to do. If a problem came up, he took care of it himself. He was capable, and he'd always done it that way.

He said the Holy Spirit convicted him that Jesus wanted to be a part of his job. He could take work problems to Jesus in prayer and get help for the problems and difficulties he faced, with the work itself and with the people he worked with and for. That had never occurred to him before for some reason, and Evie's dad wanted to change that.

Proverbs 16:3 (ESV) says, "Commit your work to the LORD, and your plans will be established." And that's exactly what Evie's dad started to do. He committed his work to the Lord. He began praying, taking his work concerns to Jesus. And God blessed him for that. Evie's dad could feel God's presence with him at work in a way he never had before.

Your work is important to God. Maybe it's just a summer job, or maybe it's your career. He wants you to "take Him to work" with you, not just leave your relationship with God at the door and dig in. He is there. He wants to help. The Bible tells us to work as though we were working for God rather than for people. God sees all that you're doing. He is there to lead you and guide you. To help you solve problems. To help in your work relationships. To be a light in an often dark place.

Evie's dad was able to share his faith with multiple coworkers when he started going to work with Jesus instead of leaving Him at the door. Work became a mission field for Evie's dad, and God was made known.

Lord, I commit my work and everything I do into Your hands. Prepare a mission field for me at work so I can be a light for You. Thanks for being with me everywhere!

BUYER'S REMORSE OR CONTENTMENT?

*I know what it is to be in need, and I know what it
is to have plenty. I have learned the secret of being
content in any and every situation, whether well fed
or hungry, whether living in plenty or in want.*
PHILIPPIANS 4:12 NIV

Jessa and I love to go shopping. She enjoys shopping for art supplies and clothes. I enjoy shopping for nice things for my home. Jessa likes to go to the stores and see all the amazing things in person. I'd rather shop online. I get ideas from Pinterest, and then I go looking for similar items that would go well in my home.

But all that shopping can get overwhelming. You see something you think you must have but then realize it's really expensive. A battle begins in your mind: *Can I make it work? Can I still buy the other things I need, like a new backpack for school and my part of the driver's ed payment?*

Buyer's remorse is a real thing. This happened when we took a tween friend with us for a day at the pool. He brought plenty of money for the entrance fee and lunch at the snack shop. But he decided that instead of swimming, he wanted to get some sweets at the snack bar. He went back several times. Then at lunch, he came over and asked if we had seen his money. Turns out he'd already used it all!

Things can be incredibly tempting when they are staring

you in the face. Paul, the writer of Philippians, had a solution: learn to be content with what you have! That seems so hard, right? But Paul said there is a secret to it. The very next verse (4:13 NIV), which I bet you've heard, holds that secret: "I can do all this through him who gives me strength." When Paul saw life from God's point of view, he could be content, focusing on what he was supposed to do, not on what he felt he should have.

Many people are discontented when they are feeling lost or lonely or empty, without a purpose. That's when temptations are hard to resist. So what do you do to get filled up? *You can do all things through Christ who gives you strength.* You take your thoughts and feelings to God and get His point of view. Let Him give your life meaning and purpose and contentment.

Lord Jesus, I need Your strength to resist temptation and be content with what I have. Fill my life with purpose and meaning. Help me seek You in all things.

THE ARMOR OF GOD

Finally, be strong in the Lord and in his mighty power. Put on the full armor of God, so that you can take your stand against the devil's schemes. For our struggle is not against flesh and blood, but against the rulers, against the authorities, against the powers of this dark world and against the spiritual forces of evil in the heavenly realms.

EPHESIANS 6:10–12 NIV

Jessa ran out the door to volleyball practice and realized she had forgotten something extremely important: knee pads. Volleyball players dive for the ball on a regular basis. Without those knee pads, your knees would be toast! A recent rule change allows volleyball players to use their feet to kick the ball. It says, "If a volleyball player determines their only hope for a dig or reaching the ball is with his or her foot, then it is perfectly acceptable to make that play." This made me wonder if the rule change was because of too many knee injuries! Whatever the reason for the rule change, volleyball players must have their knee pads on or they aren't protected from a frequent source of injury. They won't play without them.

The armor of God is like that for Christians. You can't leave home without it! And if it's that important, you definitely need to know more about it.

Let's start at the beginning. Why do we need armor in the first place? The Bible tells us that we have an enemy. He is known as the father of lies (John 8:44), the accuser who makes us feel bad about ourselves (Revelation 12:10), and the ruler of darkness (Ephesians 6:12).

Colossians 2:15 (AMP) tells us, "When He had disarmed the rulers and authorities [those supernatural forces of evil operating against us], He made a public example of them. . .having triumphed over them through the cross." Because of Jesus, Satan doesn't have any real power over you! But even though the enemy knows he's been defeated, he's still trying his best to get into your head and discourage you so much that you won't be able to live for Jesus. First Peter 5:8 (NIV) says, "Be alert and of sober mind. Your enemy the devil prowls around like a roaring lion looking for someone to devour."

That's why Jesus wants you to stay alert and put on your armor. Over the next couple of days, we're going to talk more about this armor and how it's used. It's even more important than a volleyball player's knee pads. Trust me.

Lord God, I'm so thankful that You've given me weapons to protect myself from the enemy's schemes. Help me to be alert. Help me not to fall for his tricks as I stay close to You!

PUT ON YOUR BELT

*Therefore, put on every piece of God's armor so you
will be able to resist the enemy in the time of evil.
Then after the battle you will still be standing firm.
Stand your ground, putting on the belt of truth.*
EPHESIANS 6:13–14 NLT

Before belts became a fashion statement, they were designed simply to hold up your pants. One of the knock-knock jokes we used to say when my kids were little was this:

"Knock-knock?"

"Who's there?"

"Pencil."

"Pencil who?"

"Pencil fall down if you don't wear a belt!"

Yep, pants will fall down if you don't wear a belt.

One piece of armor God gives you is called the "belt of truth." A soldier in battle during Bible times had a belt to secure all the other pieces of his armor. Have you ever seen those special belts that people wear when they do a lot of heavy lifting? They are thick and wide for lots of core support. It may have been something like that.

The belt of truth helps keep everything in the right place. When you are firmly grounded in truth from God's Word, you can stand strong, and you won't believe the enemy's lies about who you are or who God is.

Truth from God's Word is what you need to secure your

life—and everything about it. Feelings come and go, but God's truth never changes.

I watched a sad documentary recently about a girl who had a great home life and wonderful parents. But she started watching YouTube videos in high school that had her questioning who she was. She found encouragement to change her gender on social media. So she went through with it. But several years later, after her brain had matured and she'd become an adult, she realized what a terrible mistake she had made. And there was no way to undo what she had done to her body.

She wasn't grounded in truth, and so when she was encouraged to make life-altering changes to her body because of her temporary feelings, she went for it.

As a teenager in today's culture, it's so important to know the truth and let it inform your feelings instead of the other way around.

How can you do this? Spend time in God's Word every day! Memorize scripture and watch as the Holy Spirit brings it to mind right when you need it. We'll talk more about this tomorrow.

Can you picture yourself putting on God's armor? Start with the belt of truth.

Lord, I want to secure Your truth around me like a belt! Let it hold me up when I'm tempted to agree with the culture or my feelings. Help me get into Your Word and apply it to my life.

*Jesus said to him, "I am the [only] Way [to God]
and the [real] Truth and the [real] Life; no one
comes to the Father but through Me."*

JOHN 14:6 AMP

A popular video game app allows players to "travel" between the real world and virtual reality to catch characters in a worldwide game. If you have the app installed on your phone, it will buzz when you get close to one of these characters when you are out and about. If you can catch one of them, you get special rewards. It's an addicting game. And, as it turns out, can be quite dangerous. Traffic accidents and deaths have occurred because of this game. People get sucked into the virtual world, and they forget that real life is happening around them—like cars on the road coming at them!

Virtual reality might be fun for an hour or two, but if you spend more time in your virtual world instead of the real one, you miss out on the abundant and real life that Jesus has for you.

Jesus is the "real" truth and the "real" life. If you find yourself heading to the virtual, online, or streaming world to binge on shows and games as a form of escape from your life, it's time to figure out why that is and what to do about it.

Jesus has an epic adventure planned for your life! If you're feeling bored and like your spiritual life is anything but adventurous, listen up. The enemy wants you to feel bored and distracted so that you will numb out on mindless entertainment, social media, and the virtual world instead of being effective in the amazing world God has made.

What can you do about it? Find out the truth about who you are and start living it! Here is the truth from God's Word.

* I am a precious child of the Father (Isaiah 43:7; John 1:12; Galatians 3:26).

* I am loved (Jeremiah 31:3; John 3:16; 1 John 4:9–10).

* I am chosen (Colossian 3:12; 1 Peter 2:9).

* I am free and clean in the blood of Christ (Galatians 5:1; 1 John 1:7).

* He has rescued me from darkness and has brought me into His kingdom (Colossians 1:13).

* I am a friend of Christ (John 15:15).

* I am complete in Christ (Colossians 2:9–10).

* Nothing can separate me from God's love (Romans 8:38–39).

* God knows me intimately (Psalm 139).

* God is for me, not against me (Romans 8:31).

Go back and circle the truths that have special meaning for you. Begin telling yourself these truths every day.

God, please help me to know the truth of who I am and who You are so that I can stand firm against the enemy's lies and distractions.

THE BREASTPLATE OF RIGHTEOUSNESS

So stand firm and hold your ground, having tightened the wide band of truth (personal integrity, moral courage) around your waist and having put on the breastplate of righteousness (an upright heart).
EPHESIANS 6:14 AMP

In Bible times, a breastplate was a strong piece of iron worn over the chest to protect the heart and other major organs. Spiritually speaking, protecting your heart is extremely important. Why is your heart worth protecting? Proverbs 4:23 (NIV) tells us the answer: "Above all else, guard your heart, for everything you do flows from it."

"Everything you do flows from it." Cara, whom you'll learn more about on page 92, gave her heart to her high school boyfriend. She gave her unguarded heart away, and her actions followed. Feelings, thoughts, and emotions tend to drive behavior. That's why protecting your heart with truth is so important.

You've probably heard it said of someone that they "wear their heart on their sleeve." That means everyone can see what's happening in their unguarded heart. A better thing to do would be to protect that area under the breastplate of righteousness, allowing Jesus the first and deepest look at your feelings, thoughts, and emotions.

Let's talk about righteousness for a minute. Righteousness

means being right with God. First Corinthians 1:30 (NLT) tells us that "Christ made us right with God; he made us pure and holy, and he freed us from sin." Because of all that Jesus did for us in his death and resurrection, God sees us as pure and holy. Jesus took all of the punishment for our mistakes. We are not held eternally responsible for sin. So that means we are right with God, or righteous. You have an "upright heart" because of Jesus.

Romans 4:22–24 (NLT) says, "Because of Abraham's faith, God counted him as righteous. And when God counted him as righteous, it wasn't just for Abraham's benefit. It was recorded for our benefit too, assuring us that God will also count us as righteous if we believe in him, the one who raised Jesus our Lord from the dead."

The story of Abraham's life and faith was recorded in the Bible so that we could learn from it. Just as God counted Abraham as righteous, He counts us as righteous too—if we believe in Him!

So let's put all this together. When you remind yourself of this truth every day—that you are righteous in and because of Jesus—you are protecting your heart from lies and discouragement. You don't have to work hard to take your sins away! That battle has been won by Jesus Himself. Can you imagine yourself putting on the breastplate of righteousness to protect your heart as you pray?

Jesus, thank You for making me righteous before God. Please protect my heart from sin and discouragement.

WALKING WITH SHOES OF PEACE

For shoes, put on the peace that comes from the
Good News so that you will be fully prepared.
EPHESIANS 6:15 NLT

Good shoes are very important. Our family went to Disney World, where the average person is known to walk about ten miles a day. Some say that calories don't count in Disney World, like magic. But what's really happening is that most people walk off everything they eat while they're there! I did not have good shoes. I thought I did. They were fine for my everyday use. But you find out how good your shoes really are when you walk for miles and miles and miles. By the end of the first day, my feet were covered in blisters. And the blisters covered the bottoms of my feet so that I could not walk at all without excruciating pain. It felt like a fire erupted on the bottom of my feet every time I tried to step down. I ended up in a wheelchair for two days at the parks. This caused stress for me and my family since I needed to be pushed everywhere.

Walkers and runners and soldiers know how important it is to have good shoes. Have you ever seen a pair of athletic shoes with spikes on them? These are used to help athletes get a firm grip on the track. Soldiers in Bible times had spikes on their shoes to keep their feet firmly planted in the ground. God tells us that spiked spiritual shoes are an important piece of armor for believers to wear so that we can stand firm.

The Amplified Bible explains today's verse like this: "And having strapped on your feet the gospel of peace in preparation [to face the enemy with firm-footed stability and the readiness produced by the good news]." The shoes of peace can help you walk in the ways of Jesus and protect you from going down a dangerous path. Jesus came to show you the way to peace with God. He wants you to live in that peace and share it with others.

Romans 10:15 (NLT) says, "And how will anyone go and tell them without being sent? That is why the Scriptures say, 'How beautiful are the feet of messengers who bring good news!' "

As you walk toward others in love and peace, ask Jesus to give you courage to share His peace with others.

Check out these two verses that also talk to us about walking:

* "Even when I walk through the darkest valley, I will not be afraid, for you are close beside me" (Psalm 23:4 NLT).

* "When they walk through the Valley of Weeping, it will become a place of refreshing springs" (Psalm 84:6 NLT).

Picture yourself putting on the shoes of peace as you pray.

Jesus, thank You for Your great gift of peace. Help me to walk in Your ways.

THE SHIELD OF FAITH

In addition to all this, take up the shield of faith, with which you can extinguish all the flaming arrows of the evil one.
EPHESIANS 6:16 NIV

As followers of Jesus, we're in a daily battle. Spiritual warfare is going on all around us, whether we choose to see it or not. In 2 Kings 6, Elisha asked God to open the eyes of his servant, who couldn't see with eyes of faith. It's a really cool story. And it's true! In verse 16 (NIV), Elisha said to his servant, "Don't be afraid. . . . Those who are with us are more than those who are with them." The Lord opened the servant's eyes, and suddenly he could see hills full of "chariots of fire"—God's unseen army sent to help them.

The Bible is full of real-life stories of what's going on in the spiritual realm that you can't see with your physical eyes. You need eyes of faith. Faith is believing in things unseen (Hebrews 11:1). You also need a *shield* of faith.

The shield of faith protects you from enemy arrows. In Bible times, a soldier would have a large shield big enough to hide his whole body behind. It was made of leather and iron. The soldier would soak his shield in water before a battle, and this would put out the fiery arrows the enemy would shoot his way.

One could read that and think, *Oh my goodness. That sounds so heavy! How could I ever lift that up to protect myself?* Thankfully, the Bible tells us that God Himself is our shield:

* "But you, Lord, are a shield around me, my glory, the One who lifts my head high" (Psalm 3:3 NIV).

* "The Lord is my strength and my shield; my heart trusts in him, and he helps me" (Psalm 28:7 NIV).

* "The Lord is my rock, my fortress, and my savior; my God is my rock, in whom I find protection. He is my shield, the power that saves me, and my place of safety" (Psalm 18:2 NLT).

* "We wait in hope for the Lord; he is our help and our shield" (Psalm 33:20 NIV).

* "My shield is God Most High, who saves the upright in heart" (Psalm 7:10 NIV).

Our enemy likes to throw fiery arrows at us to try to pierce our hearts and get us to believe his lies. Our shield of faith reminds us of who we are in Christ and puts out those fiery darts. Thankfully, we don't have to exhaust ourselves holding up a heavy shield on our own.

Make Psalm 18:35 (NLT) your prayer today:

Lord, "You have given me your shield of victory. Your right hand supports me; your help has made me great." Thank You for being my shield and my place of safety.

THE HELMET OF SALVATION

Put on salvation as your helmet.
EPHESIANS 6:17 NLT

If you grow up in the country, you will rarely see kids wearing helmets while riding bikes. But if you live in the city or suburbs, every biker seems to be wearing a helmet. We've lived both places multiple times. Country, no helmets. City, helmets. When we lived in a suburban Colorado neighborhood, every time our kids had a checkup, our pediatrician made sure to remind them to wear their biking helmets. Now that we're back in a rural area, we haven't heard anything about helmets.

Recently, a group of boys in our rural area went on a twenty-mile bike trail ride. One of the boys had moved here from a bigger city. He brought a helmet, but none of his friends had one on, so he left his in the car. Right around that time, a young teen boy in our area who was riding his bike to the park pulled out in front of a car and was hit. He was not wearing a helmet, and he got hurt pretty badly. If you're riding a bike in an area where there is regular traffic, a helmet can save your life.

As you go out into this world, you'll have to fight against a lot of messages and lies that you may be tempted to believe—especially when some of your friends might be believing them. The helmet of salvation helps protect you from damaging lies in your mind. This is a big deal!

So put on your helmet of salvation every day and remind yourself of the truth: you are saved from the punishment of sin, you have God's own Spirit and power alive inside you, and you are set apart by God as His beloved daughter. That's the truth you need to wear on your head every single day of your life. Let it seep into your mind and change the way you live and respond to the world around you.

First Corinthians 2:16 (AMP) says, "For who has known the mind and purposes of the Lord, so as to instruct Him? But we have the mind of Christ [to be guided by His thoughts and purposes]."

As you picture yourself putting on the helmet of salvation, ask God to help you believe His truth and to think His thoughts, to "have the mind of Christ." Ask Him to protect your mind and keep it pure.

Thank You for my salvation, Lord. I know it cost You everything. Please protect my mind as I put my helmet of salvation on every day. Guide me by putting Your thoughts and purposes in my mind.

THE SWORD OF THE SPIRIT

And take the sword of the Spirit, which is the word of God.
EPHESIANS 6:17 NLT

Think about a battle scene that you've watched in a movie. What happens when one soldier loses his sword? He goes on the defense, right? He grasps at anything he can get his hands on to use as a weapon. He hides behind whatever he can find. A soldier without a sword isn't going to be able to do very much to win the battle. He is defenseless against the enemy's sword.

The sword of the Spirit is your God-given weapon. The sword of the Spirit is God's Word. Second Timothy 3:16–17 (NIV) tells us more about this: "All Scripture is God-breathed and is useful for teaching, rebuking, correcting and training in righteousness, so that the servant of God may be thoroughly equipped for every good work."

This is how Jesus Himself defeated Satan in Matthew 4:1–11. Every time Satan would tempt Him, Jesus replied with scripture. Take a look at verses 3 and 4 in the New Living Translation: "During that time the devil came and said to him, 'If you are the Son of God, tell these stones to become loaves of bread.' But Jesus told him, 'No! The Scriptures say, "People do not live by bread alone, but by every word that comes from the mouth of God." ' "

Jesus was teaching us that we can use the sword of the Spirit—the Word of God—to defend ourselves from Satan's attacks. In a paper written about spiritual warfare, Christian counselor Kevin Nass says that Jesus could have easily told Satan, "Get away from Me. I'm God," and Satan would have had to obey Him. But Jesus didn't do this because that's not something that humans can do.

Instead, Jesus modeled for us exactly what to do when Satan starts coming after us: defend ourselves with truth from God's Word. Get out those "I am" statements (found on page 79) and other truths from the Bible, and declare them out loud!

James 4:7 (NIV) says, "Submit yourselves, then, to God. Resist the devil, and he will flee from you." When you're attacked by lies from the enemy, submit yourself to God first. Align yourself with His truth. Ask for His covering. Put on the armor of God. Then you are prepared to resist the devil, using the sword of the Spirit as your weapon. And what happens next? "He will flee." He has to. And you can remind yourself and the enemy of that truth when he starts coming after your mind and heart.

As you picture yourself holding your sword, ask God to help you understand and remember His words so you can use them well against your enemy.

Thank You, Lord, for giving me Your armor of protection. Please show me how to use this armor well.

ARMOR EVERY DAY

*And pray in the Spirit on all occasions with all kinds of
prayers and requests. With this in mind, be alert and
always keep on praying for all the Lord's people.*
EPHESIANS 6:18 NIV

Praying and putting on the armor of God every day is so important! *The Message* paraphrase of the Bible helps us understand
a bit more: "Be prepared. You're up against far more than you
can handle on your own. Take all the help you can get, every
weapon God has issued, so that when it's all over but the shouting
you'll still be on your feet. Truth, righteousness, peace, faith, and
salvation are more than words. Learn how to apply them. You'll
need them throughout your life. God's Word is an indispensable
weapon. . . . Pray for your brothers and sisters. Keep your eyes
open. Keep each other's spirits up so that no one falls behind
or drops out" (Ephesians 6:13–18).

Grab your journal or a piece of notebook paper and sketch
a quick picture of yourself. Label which piece of armor goes
over what body part. If you're an artist, do your thing! If not, a
stick figure and words will do. Now make a copy for your wall, to
put next to your mirror. As you're getting ready in the morning,
start your day in prayer. Picture yourself putting on each piece
of armor as you pray and before you head out the door.

Today's scripture tells us to "pray in the Spirit on all occasions with all kinds of prayers." Start a prayer in the morning and
let prayer be a part of everything you do—a conversation with

God you start in the morning and finish before you fall asleep.

Romans 8:26–27 (NLT) tells us more about praying in the Spirit: "And the Holy Spirit helps us in our weakness. For example, we don't know what God wants us to pray for. But the Holy Spirit prays for us with groanings that cannot be expressed in words. And the Father who knows all hearts knows what the Spirit is saying, for the Spirit pleads for us believers in harmony with God's own will."

When you don't know what to do or what to pray or who to pray for, the Holy Spirit helps! As you submit yourself to God in prayer, things change as the Holy Spirit gets to work. James 5:16 (NLT) says, "Confess your sins to each other and pray for each other so that you may be healed. The earnest prayer of a righteous person has great power and produces wonderful results."

Lord, teach me to pray and put on my armor every day. Thank You that the Holy Spirit is helping me in my weakness. I am righteous because of Christ alone, and I trust that my prayers have power. That is awesome!

GUARD YOUR HEART

Above all else, guard your heart,
for everything you do flows from it.
PROVERBS 4:23 NIV

Cara was head over heels in love with a boy she met in high school. She felt like she was powerless against his charms. They both came from difficult home situations. And she compromised herself in every way with this boy. A friend invited her to church, and she accepted Jesus there. But the boy she loved went to the same church. Turns out he wasn't very serious about his faith. They stayed together until the boy went away to college, and then Cara hardly heard from him again. Until summer when things started all over again. He used Cara for a summer fling when he was home and forgot about her when he left. This went on until he graduated from college and married someone else.

Cara had given her heart completely to that boy, and she secretly believed that he would marry her. But when he betrayed her, she was devastated. She hadn't been treated well at home, so she didn't know what it was like to be treated with love and respect from a man. She hadn't learned to guard her heart.

This story is sad but true. And it happens a lot. The book of Proverbs tells us to guard our hearts above all else. Why is this so important? Because "everything you do flows from it."

It's been said that "the heart wants what it wants," and people can make very foolish choices if they are just following the whims of their unguarded hearts.

So how do you guard your heart? First, you have to make sure that you're not just giving it away to anyone cute who comes along. Does your heart belong to Jesus first? Then make sure that anyone who wants to have your heart has to go through Jesus first to get to it.

Colossians 3:3 (NLT) says, "For you died to this life, and your real life is hidden with Christ in God." Something to memorize and get in the habit of repeating to yourself is this: "I am hidden with Christ in God." Go ahead, say it out loud! "I am hidden with Christ in God."

Your heart is safely tucked away with Christ in God. If a gentleman wants to pursue your heart someday, let him ask God for permission first. If the guy is unwilling to do that, then you know that isn't a relationship worth engaging in.

So guard your heart, friend. You'll definitely regret *not* guarding it!

Lord, I'm so thankful that I'm tucked safely away in Your arms. Please teach me to guard my heart. Help me not to get carried away by my emotions when it comes to the boys I like. Give me wisdom when the time comes for me to pursue a relationship.

GOD'S ARTWORK

*For we are God's masterpiece. He has created
us anew in Christ Jesus, so we can do the
good things he planned for us long ago.*
EPHESIANS 2:10 NLT

A friend of ours is an extremely talented artist. She gave our daughter art lessons for several months. While Jessa was learning to work with paint on canvas, our friend gave us a tip that we had never realized before. If you finish your painting and you don't like how it turned out, you can just paint over it and start again! You can always paint over your old canvases.

That reminded me of life. There are definitely seasons of my life that I regret. Sometimes shame even tries to rear its ugly head and tell me that God can't use me anymore because I've made such a mess of things in my past. Have you ever felt like that? Like maybe you've messed up too badly and you're too embarrassed to try again?

But this verse challenges that lie that I'm tempted to believe. I'm God's masterpiece. You are God's masterpiece. He created us to do good things, and He planned them out long ago.

Take a look at the Amplified Bible version of today's verse: "For we are His workmanship [His own master work, a work of art], created in Christ Jesus [reborn from above—spiritually transformed, renewed, ready to be used] for good works, which God prepared [for us] beforehand [taking paths which He set], so that we would walk in them [living the good life which He prearranged and made ready for us]."

God is creating a beautiful work of art in each of our lives. There might be some ugly stuff on the canvas, but God is the Master Creator, and He can take all of our regrets and mistakes and paint something lovely and beautiful and useful with it and over it.

What comes to mind when you think of God creating you anew into a master work of art? What happens to all of those past regrets and failures as you imagine Him as the Master artist of your life?

Take these questions to God in prayer.

Lord, there are seasons in my life that make me cringe. I feel shame over my past failures and mistakes. I'm ashamed of how I handled things, and I feel like I embarrassed myself and You. I bring all of those times to You now. Will You create something useful and beautiful out of them? Please take away my guilt and shame. Wash me in Your grace. Renew me. Transform me spiritually in Christ Jesus. I trust that You set the path for my life and that it is good. Take my life and use me to bring You glory and honor and praise!

CLAY IN THE FATHER'S HANDS

The Lord will accomplish that which concerns me;
Your [unwavering] lovingkindness, O Lord, endures
forever—Do not abandon the works of Your own hands.
PSALM 138:8 AMP

Yesterday, we talked about being God's artwork. Isaiah 64:8 (NIV) says, "Yet you, Lord, are our Father. We are the clay, you are the potter; we are all the work of your hand."

Now take a look at Jeremiah 18:1–6 (NIV):

> *This is the word that came to Jeremiah from the Lord: "Go down to the potter's house, and there I will give you my message." So I went down to the potter's house, and I saw him working at the wheel. But the pot he was shaping from the clay was marred in his hands; so the potter formed it into another pot, shaping it as seemed best to him.*
>
> *Then the word of the Lord came to me. He said, "Can I not do with you, Israel, as this potter does?" declares the Lord. "Like clay in the hand of the potter, so are you in my hand, Israel."*

God is the Master Creator, remember? He is creating a beautiful work of art out of our lives. God can use a lump of marred clay and form it into something useful in His hands.

Have you ever tried to make something out of a lump of clay? It's hard work. Experienced potters make it look easy. But if you ever had to make something out of clay during middle school art class, you know what I'm talking about. It's not easy to make something useful and beautiful. In fact, the majority of our class made stuff that only a mother could love.

But God knows exactly what He's doing with your life. He is carefully and lovingly shaping and molding you as you yield to His work in your life. There are times of pain and fire that every lump of clay has to go through. He trims a little here. He pushes a little there. There is a dry period where all you do is wait patiently. Then a glaze is applied and the clay is put into a kiln of high heat. This makes the clay container durable and impenetrable. He is making you into something wonderful!

And He will not abandon the works of His own hands! How do we know? Check it out:

* "I am convinced and confident of this very thing, that He who has begun a good work in you will [continue to] perfect and complete it until the day of Christ Jesus [the time of His return]" (Philippians 1:6 AMP).

* "The one who calls you is faithful, and he will do it" (1 Thessalonians 5:24 NIV).

Lord, I trust You to shape me and mold me into something useful.

CALLING ON GOD

*On the day I called, You answered me; and You made me
bold and confident with [renewed] strength in my life.*
PSALM 138:3 AMP

Back before cell phones were invented, most people had a land-line in their home with a long coiled cord. Sometimes families would have only one phone. If you were fortunate, you had a cordless phone that you could walk around the house with. Otherwise, you were tied to the wall. Teenage girls would beg for their parents to let them have a phone in their own room.

Before "call waiting" was invented (ask your parents!), you might pick up the phone to call a friend and you would get an annoying busy signal. You'd hang up and have to try again later. But if your friend was talking to someone else for a long time, you had to wait and wait to get through. Texting was not a thing. You simply had to wait. And you still weren't guaranteed that you would ever get through to your friend the same day. And if your brother or mom needed to use the phone too? It was a lesson in patience for sure! All this waiting could be very frustrating if you had something important you needed to talk to someone about or if you missed school and were trying to get the assignments for the day.

Times sure have changed! Now, all we have to do is pick up our phone and text our message to whomever we want and they get it immediately. They may or may not answer quickly, though. And that's okay. But with God, we can trust that He is always listening and He answers on the day we call to Him. We don't have to wait to be assured of His love for us. We don't have to wonder if He'll ever pick up. He is thinking of us always, and He is faithful! Take a look:

* "The faithful love of the Lord never ends! His mercies never cease" (Lamentations 3:22 NLT).

* "Know therefore that the Lord your God is God; he is the faithful God, keeping his covenant of love to a thousand generations of those who love him and keep his commandments" (Deuteronomy 7:9 NIV).

* "You can be sure of this: The Lord set apart the godly for himself. The Lord will answer when I call to him" (Psalm 4:3 NLT).

* "The eyes of the Lord watch over those who do right, and his ears are open to their prayers. But the Lord turns his face against those who do evil" (1 Peter 3:12 NLT).

Lord, I'm so thankful that You hear me when I call. Help me to learn to come to You with everything and listen as You respond. I know all things are possible when I call on You!

DAVID'S REGRETS

Nathan said to David, "You are the man! This is what the LORD, the God of Israel, says: 'I anointed you king over Israel, and I delivered you from the hand of Saul. . . . Why did you despise the word of the LORD by doing what is evil in his eyes? You struck down Uriah the Hittite with the sword and took his wife to be your own. You killed him with the sword of the Ammonites.'"

2 SAMUEL 12:7, 9 NIV

Let's take a look at some of the people in the Bible and what we can learn from their biggest regrets. We'll start with David. Here's a brief summary of David's life: He was a shepherd boy who killed the giant Goliath with a stone. He was a poet and musician who wrote many psalms. He was a soldier who became known as the greatest king of Israel. And he is an ancestor of Jesus Christ.

But David sinned greatly. He wanted someone else's wife for his own, so he had Bathsheba's husband murdered. Yes, this great man who was called "a man after God's own heart" lied, committed adultery, and had a man killed.

God sent the prophet Nathan to show David his sin, and David repented. He wrote Psalm 51 in response: "Have mercy on me, O God, according to your unfailing love; according to your great compassion blot out my transgressions. Wash away all my iniquity and cleanse me from my sin. For I know my transgressions, and my sin is always before me. Against you, you only, have I sinned and done what is evil in your sight; so you are right in your verdict and justified when you judge" (verses 1–4 NIV).

David owned his mistakes and regrets. He repented and turned to God: "Create in me a pure heart, O God, and renew a steadfast spirit within me. Do not cast me from your presence or take your Holy Spirit from me. Restore to me the joy of your salvation and grant me a willing spirit, to sustain me. Then I will teach transgressors your ways, so that sinners will turn back to you" (Psalm 51:10–13 NIV).

David's story shows us that sinners can turn back to God in repentance and be forgiven. The prophet Nathan told David that God had taken away his sin. A lot of natural consequences happened because of David's sin, though. His son died, and calamity followed him. But David learned from his mistakes, and he didn't keep making them. He followed after God's heart until the end.

God, create in me a pure heart too.
Renew my spirit and cleanse me from sin.
Thank You for Your forgiveness and love.
Help me become a girl after Your own heart.

ESAU'S REGRET

Make sure that no one is immoral or godless like Esau,
who traded his birthright as the firstborn son for a
single meal. You know that afterward, when he wanted
his father's blessing, he was rejected. It was too late for
repentance, even though he begged with bitter tears.
HEBREWS 12:16–17 NLT

Esau's story is told in the book of Genesis. His parents were Isaac and Rebekah. His twin brother was Jacob. The story is a baffling one. Esau grew up a skilled hunter. He was out hunting one day and came home famished. Jacob was there, cooking some stew. Esau was desperate for some and asked Jacob for a bowlful. But Jacob wanted a trade. Maybe Esau thought it was a joke at first when Jacob asked for Esau's birthright in exchange for stew? But that's what Jacob wanted. And Esau was so hungry he agreed.

A birthright was something special. It was a right of the firstborn son that included financial and leadership blessings. Esau gave all that away in a moment of weakness. His growling stomach ruled his mind. You can see how this turned out in Genesis 27. Isaac was on his deathbed, and Jacob received the birthright blessing instead of Esau (through deceitful means all the way around!).

Verse 34 (NLT) says, "When Esau heard his father's words, he let out a loud and bitter cry. 'Oh my father, what about me? Bless me too!' he begged."

It was too late at that point. A man's word was binding, and the blessing had already been given to Jacob. Esau was full of regret at this point for his foolish choices. He wasn't thinking about the consequences of his actions; he just wanted what he wanted when he wanted it! Ever felt that way? What Esau needed was some impulse control.

An impulse is a sudden urge to do something. Impulse control is the ability to control those sudden urges. You've felt this way around birthday time before, I bet. Your mom makes a tasty-looking cake, and it's just sitting there waiting to be enjoyed. You have a sudden impulse to have a little taste. Or you have a sudden impulse to do something you know is wrong, like lying to get out of trouble. It's something that happens suddenly, and you act without thinking about the consequences.

How do you get "impulse control"? Thankfully self-control is one of the fruits of the Spirit (Galatians 5:23). And 2 Timothy 1:7 (NIV) tells us, "For the Spirit God gave us does not make us timid, but gives us power, love and self-discipline."

As you follow Jesus and allow His Spirit to lead and teach you, self-control is a fruit that starts growing in you.

Lord, help me learn from Esau's life. Please grow the fruit of self-control in my heart and mind.

PETER'S REGRET

At that moment the Lord turned and looked at Peter.
Suddenly, the Lord's words flashed through Peter's
mind: "Before the rooster crows tomorrow morning,
you will deny three times that you even know me."
And Peter left the courtyard, weeping bitterly.
LUKE 22:61–62 NLT

Simon Peter was one of Jesus' twelve disciples. He was a fisherman and a close friend of Jesus. He was well known for being outspoken and impulsive. He was the one who started to walk on water with Jesus until he looked around, got scared, and started to sink (take a look at that story in Matthew 14). And fear led to Peter's greatest regret.

So what happened? Jesus was arrested, Peter ran away, and later he denied that he even knew Jesus. Not once, not twice, but three times. Jesus told him ahead of time that this would happen, and Peter was sure it wouldn't. But Peter was afraid. Fear can cause you to make some crazy choices. When he realized what he'd done, and it had happened just as Jesus said it would, he wept bitterly.

We can learn a lot from what happened with Peter. Peter was a pretty good guy. He loved Jesus. He didn't intend to sin or betray Jesus. He thought he would never do such a thing. But Peter was an impulsive dude. Scripture seems to suggest that Peter just did and said whatever came to mind without thinking it through. He had a lot of spiritual growing up to do.

Jesus had some good plans and purposes for Peter (he was also called Simon). In Luke 22:31–34 (NIV), Jesus said, "Simon, Simon, Satan has asked to sift all of you as wheat. But I have prayed for you, Simon, that your faith may not fail. And when you have turned back, strengthen your brothers." Jesus was praying for Simon. And Jesus didn't forget him or turn his back on him even after Peter betrayed him.

Jesus had this conversation with Peter too: "Now I say to you that you are Peter (which means 'rock'), and upon this rock I will build my church, and all the powers of hell will not conquer it" (Matthew 16:18 NLT).

After Jesus rose from the grave, He went and talked with Peter. Jesus restored their relationship and gave Peter the opportunity to affirm His love for Jesus three times after betraying Him three times. Then He gave him direction for the future. Peter was a major part of establishing the early church, just as Jesus had said.

God can use you even after you've messed up. We all make mistakes. And when you turn back to Jesus, He will heal and restore you.

Jesus, thank You for Your love and grace in my life!

JUDAS' REGRET

Before the Passover celebration, Jesus knew that his hour had come to leave this world and return to his Father. He had loved his disciples during his ministry on earth, and now he loved them to the very end. It was time for supper, and the devil had already prompted Judas, son of Simon Iscariot, to betray Jesus.

JOHN 13:1–2 NLT

Judas Iscariot's regret was very different from Peter's. Both were disciples of Jesus and spent years doing ministry with Him. They worked closely with Jesus. Both had important roles as part of the ministry. They took part in the miracles. They knew Jesus well. But while Peter was restored in his relationship with Jesus after his regret, Judas' life turned out very differently.

We see here evidence that Judas was a dishonest guy: "But Judas Iscariot, the disciple who would soon betray him, said, 'That perfume was worth a year's wages. It should have been sold and the money given to the poor.' Not that he cared for the poor—he was a thief, and since he was in charge of the disciples' money, he often stole some for himself" (John 12:4–6 NLT).

This happened when Mary of Bethany anointed Jesus' feet with an expensive bottle of perfume. It was a beautiful act of worship, and Judas was upset about it. Jesus told Judas to leave her alone (John 12:7).

Judas was part of Jesus' inner circle. And yet, his heart was far from Jesus. Judas ended up betraying Jesus for thirty pieces of silver. Jesus knew Judas' heart, of course, and allowed him to stay anyway.

Read the sad conclusion to Judas' story for yourself:

> *When Judas, who had betrayed him, realized that Jesus had been condemned to die, he was filled with remorse. So he took the thirty pieces of silver back to the leading priests and the elders. "I have sinned," he declared, "for I have betrayed an innocent man."*
>
> *"What do we care?" they retorted. "That's your problem."*
>
> *Then Judas threw the silver coins down in the Temple and went out and hanged himself. (Matthew 27:3–5 NLT)*

Judas' choices led him to sin and ultimately to death at his own hand. Yet, he had lived so close to Jesus—the source of life Himself!

Over the years, this analogy has been said in many ways: being in a garage doesn't make you a car, just like being in a church doesn't make you a Christian. Just because Judas knew Jesus well doesn't meant that his heart was committed to Jesus. You can know everything there is to know about God and the Bible yet still miss the point of accepting His great love for You and committing your heart to Him. See the difference?

Jesus, I want to follow You with my whole heart!

LIFE OR DEATH

*Godly sorrow brings repentance that leads to salvation
and leaves no regret, but worldly sorrow brings death.*
2 CORINTHIANS 7:10 NIV

Peter and Judas both betrayed Jesus on the same night. Their stories are real-life examples of the choice each person has. Peter was sorry for his sin. It led him back to Jesus in repentance, and their relationship was restored. Judas was full of worldly sorrow. He felt hopeless in his regret, and he took his own life.

The Amplified Bible helps explain: "For [godly] sorrow that is in accord with the will of God produces a repentance without regret, leading to salvation; but worldly sorrow [the hopeless sorrow of those who do not believe] produces death." Repentance leads to life. Hopeless regret leads to death.

Have you ever been around someone who was caught in their sin and wasn't repentant? They're not really sorry, just sorry they got caught. Someone who is truly repentant is humble and seeks to make things right.

Acts 3:19–20 (NLT) says, "Now repent of your sins and turn to God, so that your sins may be wiped away. Then times of refreshment will come from the presence of the Lord, and he will again send you Jesus, your appointed Messiah."

True repentance brings cleansing from the presence of Jesus Himself. Second Corinthians 5:17 (NIV) says, "Therefore, if anyone is in Christ, the new creation has come: the old has gone, the new is here!"

Peter's life was transformed by the restoration and renewal that came from Jesus. He let Jesus have his whole heart, and he spent his life serving the Lord—loving God and loving others. Judas did not. He made little compromises at first that led into big sin. He let Satan have a foothold in his life. But Judas had the same access to Jesus that Peter did and the same opportunity to repent and turn from his sinful ways. He chose death.

One life of repentance changed the world, as we are still studying and learning from Peter today! His message expanded God's kingdom in countless ways throughout generations.

Romans 2:4 tells us that it is God's kindness that leads us to repentance. He is gentle with us as we make our choices. Have you chosen a life of repentance and renewal? Lay down all of your regrets, and let Him wash you with His grace and love.

Lord Jesus, show me what it means to live a life of repentance and renewal in You! Not that I'm groveling in shame every day, but that I'm humbly coming to You in my weakness to be filled with life, love, grace, mercy, and renewal. I choose You, Jesus. I choose to follow You with all my heart. Let me be a part of bringing Your kingdom on earth.

DEATHBED REGRET

"Forget the former things; do not dwell on the past.
See, I am doing a new thing! Now it springs up;
do you not perceive it? I am making a way in the
wilderness and streams in the wasteland."
Isaiah 43:18–19 NIV

Abby's uncle lived a hard and sinful life. When he was on his deathbed, Abby's mom explained the gospel to him, and all he could do was nod in agreement. Abby's mom couldn't be sure what he was trying to express, but Abby remembered the Bible passage about the two criminals hanging on the cross beside Jesus.

One of the criminals who hung there hurled insults at him: "Aren't you the Messiah? Save yourself and us!"

But the other criminal rebuked him. "Don't you fear God," he said, "since you are under the same sentence? We are punished justly, for we are getting what our deeds deserve. But this man has done nothing wrong."

Then he said, "Jesus, remember me when you come into your kingdom."

Jesus answered him, "Truly I tell you, today you will be with me in paradise." (Luke 23:39–43 NIV)

These guys were legit criminals, and they deserved their punishment. They lived sinful lives. But one of the criminals accepted Jesus, and Jesus promised him that he would be saved—even at the very last minute. How gracious and merciful our God is!

Studies have been done on what people say on their death-beds. Do you think they wish they could get a few more hours of screen time? Or a few more years to work? Those are the time wasters they regret. What they wish most is that they could have spent more time with the people they love and that they would have told them how much they loved them. They regret wasting their lives on sinful choices.

But you have your whole life ahead of you! You don't have to live in regret. Today's verse reminds us all not to dwell on those regrets we have. We can confess them to Jesus and stop carrying them around.

First John 1:9 (ESV) says, "If we confess our sins, he is faithful and just to forgive us our sins and to cleanse us from all unrighteousness." And Acts 3:19 (NLT) says, "Now repent of your sins and turn to God, so that your sins may be wiped away."

So let go of those old regrets and trust that God is doing a new thing in you. He has great plans and purposes for your life. You won't ever have to worry about deathbed regret for you will have lived your life to the fullest with God's love guiding your path.

Lord, I'm so thankful for the life You've given me!
Thanks for doing a new thing in me.
I'm committing to follow You all the days of my life.

POUR OUT YOUR HEART TO GOD

*Trust in him at all times, you people; pour out
your hearts to him, for God is our refuge.*
PSALM 62:8 NIV

One thing many people regret is pouring out their hearts to the wrong people. This happened to Elizabeth. Elizabeth and Lydia were the best of friends. They were on the same team and did just about everything together. Elizabeth and Lydia had different home lives, though. Elizabeth had an extremely dysfunctional family. Her mother had a serious illness, and the rest of the family didn't really know how to cope with that. Elizabeth often kept very busy so that she wouldn't have to spend much time at home. Lydia had a more "normal" family. Elizabeth felt like Lydia was a safe person to share her struggles with.

A few years went by, and little by little their friendship shifted. They ended up on different teams and with none of their classes together. This caused Elizabeth to feel lonely, and she wanted to talk to Lydia about it. But Lydia had made new friends with girls on her new team. And those friends weren't very accepting of Elizabeth. One day she found out that Lydia had shared a few of Elizabeth's secrets with this new group of friends. Elizabeth was devastated. She really thought she could trust Lydia. Lydia's betrayal caused a rift in their friendship that they weren't able to bounce back from, and their relationship ended.

Have you ever poured out your heart to someone and then regretted it later? This can happen with a sibling, a best friend, a boyfriend, or someone else. It happens a lot.

But you will never regret pouring out your heart to God.

There are safe and trustworthy people in the world. The Holy Spirit will help you as you seek to have relationships with good and safe people. It's healthy to share your heart with those kinds of people and to pray for and encourage one another. But getting in the habit of going to God first, before you pour out your heart to others, is a really good practice.

Ask God to give you a couple of healthy and safe friendships and a mentor to pray with and learn from. Then talk to God about what you should share with others and who you should tell. Tell Him everything first. He knows it all already, but He can help you sort out your thoughts and feelings first if you let Him. He can help you separate truth from lies. He can be a refuge for you and your tangled feelings.

Lord, thank You for being a safe place for me to pour out my heart. Help me untangle these feelings. I want to believe truth and not fall for any lies. Please provide a few safe friends to share with as You lead me.

DID YOU READ IT ON THE INTERNET?

The gullible believe anything they're told;
the prudent sift and weigh every word.
PROVERBS 14:15 MSG

There is a certain genre of nonfiction books about "useless facts." Some kids and teens love them. These books have information in them like how much the human head weighs and how many spiders people accidentally swallow every year (ew!). The books themselves are often well researched. However, most people go to the internet when they want information of any kind. And many people believe what they find.

You can research any sickness or disease. Sara had a headache, and her skin was a little itchy. Before she told her mom, she went online to see what it might be. She typed in all of her symptoms. When she finished her research, she was convinced she had a life-threatening illness and would be dead by morning.

You can go online to check out social media to see what people are doing and thinking. You can read up on politics and local events. You can find out the best thing to have for dinner. You have nearly every piece of information you could ever want at your fingertips. And for every fact and opinion, you can find a smart and knowledgeable person who says the exact opposite!

How do you sift through all of the contradictory information?

Proverbs 4:7 (NLT) says, "Getting wisdom is the wisest thing you can do! And whatever else you do, develop good judgment."

Just because you read something online doesn't make it true! God wants us to have wisdom and good judgment that come from knowing Him and His Word. The book of Proverbs has a lot to teach us about wisdom. Check out these verses:

* "Those who trust their own insight are foolish, but anyone who walks in wisdom is safe" (Proverbs 28:26 NLT).

* "Get wisdom; develop good judgment. Don't forget my words or turn away from them" (Proverbs 4:5 NLT).

As you grow up in this culture that goes online for answers to everything, consider being countercultural. What if you decided that you would go to God's Word first as your source of all wisdom? What if you committed yourself to reading His Word daily so that you could align yourself with God and His truth before heading online?

Consider printing out today's scriptures to post by your computer or have on your bedside table as a reminder to go to God's Word first before going online.

Lord, I want to align my heart and mind with Your Word. Please give me the desire to know You more and to get into Your Word first before I go online. Help me not to be gullible. Please give me wisdom as I hide Your Word in my heart.

WHEN LIFE FEELS HEAVY

"Come to me, all you who are weary and burdened,
and I will give you rest. Take my yoke upon you
and learn from me, for I am gentle and humble
in heart, and you will find rest for your souls.
For my yoke is easy and my burden is light."
MATTHEW 11:28–30 NIV

Have you ever come home from something difficult (school, sports, a day with friends that went badly, etc.) and just wanted to crawl into your bed and cry? We all have days like that. And remember, Jesus said they would come (John 16:33). Sometimes life just feels heavy.

It's in these moments that Jesus reminds us gently that He is waiting to lift the burdens off our shoulders and onto His. Psalm 23:3 (NIV) says, "He refreshes my soul. He guides me along the right paths for his name's sake."

Erica carried a heavy load. Her parents were struggling in their marriage, and they weren't sure they were going to make it. School was getting harder. Her friendships felt shallow. She felt alone. She heard about Jesus, though, and she liked what she heard. If what He said was true, He could fill her with life and love, give her a purpose, and help her through these hard times. She was willing to try trusting Him. As she got to know Jesus through His Word, she would often picture Jesus in her mind as she prayed. They would walk and talk together. Erica pictured all of her burdens and struggles in a blue backpack that

Jesus Himself would carry. And when it was time to work on one of those problems, she'd imagine Jesus sitting down with her, opening the backpack, and helping her through whatever struggle needed worked out. Erica would pray through the problem, and then she would picture Jesus packing all of those problems back up and carrying them in the blue backpack again. This prayer practice helped Erica to visualize Matthew 11:28–30.

Jesus cares about how tired and weary you are. He is there for you. He wants to help carry your load. Can you picture Him doing this while you pray?

Let *The Message* paraphrase of today's verse speak to your heart: "Are you tired? Worn out? Burned out on religion? Come to me. Get away with me and you'll recover your life. I'll show you how to take a real rest. Walk with me and work with me—watch how I do it. Learn the unforced rhythms of grace. I won't lay anything heavy or ill-fitting on you. Keep company with me and you'll learn to live freely and lightly."

Lord Jesus, I'm coming to You. I'm so glad that You offer peace and rest for my soul. I need it. Thanks for being gentle with me.

WISDOM WITH NEW FRIENDS

Leave the presence of a [shortsighted] fool, for you will not find knowledge or hear godly wisdom from his lips.
PROVERBS 14:7 AMP

Lindi was excited to start her training at the high school career center. She got to leave her high school every day and go to cosmetology school for three hours. She wasn't sure she wanted to be a cosmetologist after graduating, but she did want to learn the skill so that she would have a better idea of what to pursue when she got closer to graduation. She entered the classroom on the first day of school and was surrounded by a lot of girls she'd never met before. Lindi was good at making friends, so she wasn't worried about that. But during the first class break, many of the girls went out to smoke. Lindi took her break outside too, and while she was eating her snack, she heard several of them talking about a party they had been to just a few nights before. They were discussing the drinks they'd had and the drugs they'd tried. Lindi was disappointed and worried that she wouldn't be able to find a friend in class after all.

She went home depressed after school and talked to her mom about what happened. Her mom asked her some very thought-provoking questions. Did Lindi think she could be a light in a dark place? Could she get to know these girls and share her faith with them? Or would she be tempted to fit in with the crowd and stay silent, possibly even giving in to peer pressure just to fit in?

Lindi prayed about her dilemma. She thought she would give class a try again and see if she could make friends without compromising her values. She also had the choice to switch to an afternoon class, instead, with a different group of girls. Lindi and her mom prayed for wisdom.

What would you do in that situation? It can be really difficult to be the only Christian in a room. Sometimes God calls us into situations like that specifically to be a light in the dark. And other times, we need wisdom to avoid the company and corrupt talk of fools. Prayer is the key here.

When faced with difficult situations like this one, pray for wisdom and talk to a spiritual mentor about it too. Jesus loves all of those girls, and He wants them to know it. But going into a situation like that alone can be unwise. Ecclesiastes 4:9 (NLT) says, "Two people are better off than one, for they can help each other succeed."

Lord, when I'm faced with a difficult decision like this one, please give me wisdom. I don't want to compromise my values to fit in and make choices that I'll regret.

A STINKY MOUND OF DIRTY LAUNDRY

Do not lie to one another, seeing that you have put off the old self with its practices and have put on the new self, which is being renewed in knowledge after the image of its creator.
COLOSSIANS 3:9–10 ESV

Mondays are laundry day at our house. My daughter Jessa had a mountain of dirty laundry. She has two laundry baskets, one in her room and one in the bathroom. Each child in our house is responsible to bring their laundry downstairs on Monday mornings to be washed. Then they gather it and take it back up to their rooms and put it away on Tuesdays. It's a system that has worked well for years.

But last week was really busy. Only one of the laundry baskets made its way downstairs, and the other one in the bathroom was forgotten. That went entirely unnoticed by everyone until four days into the week. And then the problem became apparent: Jessa had no clean volleyball shorts for practice. They were left in the upstairs bathroom basket along with a mound of other stinky clothes she would need quickly if she was going to have anything to wear for the weekend. Whoops!

Yes, this is a very small regret in the grand scheme of things. But can you see how this might relate to spiritual things too? Think about lying. Someone tells a "little" fib to their parents.

It wasn't even untrue. It just wasn't the entire truth. It seemed like no big deal at the time. Nothing important. No one noticed. But then the lie caused some issues. A hole in the story became apparent. And so another lie had to be told to make the first lie believable. And on and on until all the lies became a stinking mound of dirty laundry. That's a big whoops! And it's really hard to hide a stinky mountain of dirty laundry. Someone always finds it eventually.

It's the same with lying. There's no such thing as a "little white lie." Our culture tells us it's okay to lie to spare someone's feelings or to get out of a tough situation. But the Bible tells us different. Psalm 101:7 (NLT) says, "I will not allow deceivers to serve in my house, and liars will not stay in my presence."

Lying destroys trust in relationships, and it's a big deal to God. He wants us to be honest with Him, ourselves, and one another. If you find yourself struggling with being truthful, talk to Jesus about it. Repent, turning away from sin and toward God.

Lord, I bring my sin to You in repentance. Thank You for loving and forgiving me. Thank You for making me clean. Please help me make things right and learn to be more truthful in the future.

NAILING MY REGRETS TO THE CROSS

*He made Christ who knew no sin to [judicially]
be sin on our behalf, so that in Him we would become
the righteousness of God [that is, we would be made
acceptable to Him and placed in a right relationship
with Him by His gracious lovingkindness].*
2 CORINTHIANS 5:21 AMP

Many people grow up believing that God is mad at them or perpetually disappointed. One friend told me that she believed that if she was listening to the radio when Jesus came back, she wouldn't go to heaven! She lived in fear of God. Not the healthy kind of fear and awe and reverence, but a fear of being punished by God. First John 4:17–18 (NLT) tells us all we need to know about that: "As we live in God, our love grows more perfect. So we will not be afraid on the day of judgment, but we can face him with confidence because we live like Jesus here in this world. Such love has no fear, because perfect love expels all fear. If we are afraid, it is for fear of punishment, and this shows that we have not fully experienced his perfect love."

If someone is afraid of the punishment of God, they don't yet understand what Jesus has done for them through His death and resurrection.

In the Old Testament, the Israelites were given many laws—many that seemed impossible to keep. And people broke them all the time. God gave these laws to His chosen people because they needed to know how to live in a broken world. And they needed to see and acknowledge their sin.

God is love (1 John 4:8). He is also holy and just. He does not tolerate sin. He can't be near it. So the Israelite people had to make sacrifices before God so that they could be acceptable to Him again after they sinned. They would sacrifice a lamb or some other animal for their sins.

Jesus came to fulfill all of that. "How? you ask. In Christ. God put the wrong on him who never did anything wrong, so we could be put right with God" (2 Corinthians 5:21 MSG). Jesus became our sacrificial lamb, once and for all, making us right before God forever.

Colossians 2:14 (NLT) says, "He canceled the record of the charges against us and took it away by nailing it to the cross." Jesus takes our sin and regrets and nails them to the cross. You don't need any more sacrifices to make yourself clean and acceptable before God. When God looks at you, He sees the righteousness (the rightness, the perfection) of Jesus (see Hebrews 10:12–14). You are clean and free to live a great life, with Jesus guiding you and blessing you!

Jesus, thank You for all You have done!

A GODLY TRIBE

*Some men came carrying a paralyzed man on a
sleeping mat. They tried to take him inside to Jesus,
but they couldn't reach him because of the crowd.
So they went up to the roof and took off some tiles.
Then they lowered the sick man on his mat down into
the crowd, right in front of Jesus. Seeing their faith, Jesus
said to the man, "Young man, your sins are forgiven."*
Luke 5:18–20 NLT

The true story of Jesus healing this paralyzed man is told in
three of the Gospels: Matthew, Mark, and Luke. And reading it
in each of these books gives us a better idea of what happened
from different perspectives.

One day Jesus was teaching and healing the sick in someone's
house. A group of people brought their paralyzed friend to see
Jesus. But the crowd was so large, they couldn't get through.
Houses in Bible times usually had flat roofs with stairs leading
up to them. So these guys carried their friend up to the top of
the house, over the place where Jesus was teaching, and started
making a big hole in the roof. Big enough for a man to fit through!

Can you imagine being in the room at the time? Chunks of
mud and straw were likely falling on people's heads, and then
a man was lowered through the hole to Jesus!

The Bible tells us, "When Jesus saw their faith, he said,
'Friend, your sins are forgiven.'" (Luke 5:20 NIV). Seems like kind
of a strange thing to say, right? This guy obviously needed his

legs to work, and that's why his friends went to all that trouble.

But Jesus saw the entire person. He knew exactly what his heart and body needed. One pastor commented that instead of healing his body first, Jesus wanted to reshape this man's belief around God. They lived in a culture where people with disabilities were looked down upon and believed to be disabled because of God's anger toward them. Jesus called the man friend and told him he was forgiven. He wanted this man to know he was accepted and loved by Him.

And what about this man's friends? The Amplified Bible explains, "When Jesus saw their [active] faith [springing from confidence in Him], He said, 'Man, your sins are forgiven' " (Luke 5:20).

Jesus saw the faith of this man's friends. They acted on their faith to get their friend to Jesus. Do you have friends who would break through a roof to get you to Jesus? We all need a faith community—a tribe. If you struggle with godly friendships, ask God to bring you some!

Lord, I love these true stories from the Bible. Thanks for seeing the paralyzed guy's heart and body, just as You see mine. Please help me find good and God-honoring friendships that will do things like these friends did.

LANDSCAPE FABRIC TO THE RESCUE!

Because of the privilege and authority God has given me, I give each of you this warning: Don't think you are better than you really are. Be honest in your evaluation of yourselves, measuring yourselves by the faith God has given us.
ROMANS 12:3 NLT

We have a ginormous garden on our property. When I say ginormous, I mean like a quarter of the size of a football field. We went from a tiny backyard in Colorado where I had one raised garden bed big enough for two cherry tomato plants and some flowers to a giant garden in the country where we were able to grow thirty pumpkins, loads of tomatoes, beans, carrots, onions. . .You name it, we've got it!

I had big dreams for this big space. But after years of regretting big projects and learning the hard way, I've developed some maturity in areas where I used to be weak (thanks only to the Holy Spirit at work in my life!). Here's what I knew about myself: I tend to dream big and get very excited about projects at the beginning of them. I love the "blank page"! I love the dreaming and planning process. I love to create. Putting ideas together is fun and life giving for me. It was a blast to research garden planning, sketch out my garden plan, order materials, and get it all planted.

But I have learned that I don't love the "carrying out" part of the plan. I tend to fizzle out after the project requires lots of tedious hard work. In this case, the weeding. Weeding is grueling, back-breaking work in a garden that size. There's nothing creative about it. It's just plain hard work. But there are few things a good gardener regrets more than allowing weeds to take over her carefully planned garden. I knew I wasn't going to be able to keep the weeds down myself. What was I to do?

Specialty woven landscape fabric to the rescue! I did some research on organic gardening and weed control. I was able to find some video tutorials on exactly what to use to allow moisture in and weeds out. And it worked! We're going on three years now with a mostly weed-free garden and a large, beautiful crop.

Can you relate to any of that? Do you know yourself well enough to be honest about your struggles and pitfalls? The Bible tells us to "be honest in your evaluation of yourselves." Make a list of things you struggle with. Be completely honest. Ask God for help. Allow His Spirit to come alongside you, giving you ideas and teaching you a better way.

Lord, please help me to be honest with myself and with You about my struggles. I invite Your Spirit in to teach me and show me a better way.

SERVING

*"And whoever gives one of these little ones even a
cup of cold water because he is a disciple, truly,
I say to you, he will by no means lose his reward."*
MATTHEW 10:42 ESV

The Bible has a lot to say about serving others. Check out these scriptures:

* "You, my brothers and sisters, were called to be free. But do not use your freedom to indulge the flesh; rather, serve one another humbly in love" (Galatians 5:13 NIV).

* "When God's people are in need, be ready to help them. Always be eager to practice hospitality" (Romans 12:13 NLT).

* "God has given each of you a gift from his great variety of spiritual gifts. Use them well to serve one another" (1 Peter 4:10 NLT).

* "For the poor will never cease to be in the land; therefore I command you, saying, 'You shall freely open your hand to your brother, to your needy, and to your poor in your land' " (Deuteronomy 15:11 AMP).

* "He who is gracious and lends a hand to the poor lends to the LORD, and the LORD will repay him for his good deed" (Proverbs 19:17 AMP).

* "Do not withhold good from those who deserve it when it's in your power to help them" (Proverbs 3:27 NLT).

It's important to God that we love and serve one another. And there are so many needs in our communities and in our world. Where do we begin?

The Message paraphrase helps us figure this out: "This is a large work I've called you into, but don't be overwhelmed by it. It's best to start small. Give a cool cup of water to someone who is thirsty, for instance. The smallest act of giving or receiving makes you a true apprentice. You won't lose out on a thing" (Matthew 10:41–42 MSG).

Start with a cold cup of water for someone who is thirsty. Start small. Don't let yourself be overwhelmed. Just do what you can. Do what is in your power to do. Do you have a part-time job or an allowance? How might you use a portion of that to serve someone in need? Do you know some elderly people from church? Offer to help shovel their driveway in the winter or ask what they might need that you can do. With your parents, brainstorm ways that you could serve your family and your neighbors.

You will never regret serving others, because if you lend a hand to the poor, you are actually lending to the Lord!

Lord, open my eyes and my heart to see the needs of those around me. Show me ways that I can serve my family out of love for You. Help me with ideas and energy to serve my neighbors and people at church or in my community.

LAZYBONES

One day I walked by the field of an old lazybones, and then passed the vineyard of a slob; they were overgrown with weeds, thick with thistles, all the fences broken down. I took a long look and pondered what I saw; the fields preached me a sermon and I listened: "A nap here, a nap there, a day off here, a day off there, sit back, take it easy—do you know what comes next? Just this: You can look forward to a dirt-poor life, with poverty as your permanent houseguest!"

PROVERBS 24:30–34 MSG

Jackie lost her phone. She was supposed to plug it in at the desk in the kitchen every night at 9:00, and one night she forgot. She received consequences for that because the rule in her house was to make sure the phone stayed in the kitchen overnight, and it wasn't there during that time. But it was nowhere! Or at least it seemed to be nowhere. She searched the house from top to bottom. She checked all of her backpacks, purses, and bags. She checked her closet. She went through all the couch cushions. She even looked inside the piano because she remembered watching a video tutorial of a song she wanted to learn recently. That phone had just disappeared! If only she had remembered to put it on the desk in the kitchen when she was done using it, it would have been on the desk the next morning when she went looking for it.

This happens with shoes too. If you don't put them back in your closet, they end up walking off on their own it seems.

And clothes. You take your favorite hoodie off and put it on a chair, and then you never see it again. It happens. Putting things where they belong is the best way to find them when you need them, right?

Everyone regrets losing their favorite hoodie, shoes, and especially their phone. It's one thing to be a little absent-minded and forgetful. (We all have days like that!) It's another to be lazy. A lazy person is constantly leaving their stuff everywhere because they just don't feel like putting it away. Laziness might not seem like a big deal when it comes to clothes and shoes, but if it becomes a habit in your life, it can be really hard to break when you get older—and it matters. Like this guy mentioned in Proverbs. His laziness caused his poverty. There's nothing wrong with taking a much-deserved rest and a nap when you need it or being a little absent-minded here and there. But making it a lifestyle will cause you harm in the long run.

Do you struggle with laziness? Ask God for awareness and help.

Lord, I don't want to be a lazy person. Show me the places in my character that need some work.

PROCRASTINATION

*But the Holy Spirit produces this kind of fruit
in our lives: love, joy, peace, patience, kindness,
goodness, faithfulness, gentleness, and self-
control. There is no law against these things!*
GALATIANS 5:22–23 NLT

Hannah had a huge paper due for her high school English class. She knew the deadline was three weeks away. She had to read a hefty book and then write a long report about it. She was a busy girl. She had several other activities and events going on at the same time, but she knew she could handle them if she was careful with her time management.

Days went by, though, and she allowed herself to get distracted. She wanted to chat with her friends instead of reading the book. Then there were days that she just didn't feel like reading at all. So she didn't. One week went by, then another. She only had the book halfway read. Finally, she got to the last three days before the deadline and she was in a complete panic. There was no way she could finish her book and write a paper in that amount of time. Not unless she gave up eating and sleeping.

Hannah was definitely regretting her procrastination choices at this point. Leaving things until the very last minute is a character issue for many people. If you struggle with this—and trust me, you are not alone!—the antidote is faithfulness.

Faithfulness is one of the fruits of the Spirit. So the great news is that if you don't have very much fruit in this area, the Holy

Spirit can grow that in you! You just need some good soil. Good soil is weed-free and ready for seeds to be planted. Matthew 13:23 (NLT) says, "The seed that fell on good soil represents those who truly hear and understand God's word and produce a harvest of thirty, sixty, or even a hundred times as much as had been planted!"

First, go to Jesus and repent of your procrastination choices. Procrastination causes stress for yourself and those around you. Ask Jesus to highlight any weeds you have growing in your heart and to pull them out. Now you have space for some good seed to be planted. Then ask the Holy Spirit to start growing good fruits in you, especially the fruit of faithfulness. Luke 16:10 (NLT) tells us, "If you are faithful in little things, you will be faithful in large ones."

As you cooperate with the process of the Holy Spirit growing faithfulness in your heart, get ready for a huge harvest!

Lord, I want to be faithful in small things so that I'll eventually be faithful with big things. Please pull out the weeds that are getting in the way and help me to cooperate with that process. Plant faithfulness in me and let it grow.

REGRETTING THE RIP-OFF

*Committed and persistent work pays off;
get-rich-quick schemes are ripoffs.*
PROVERBS 28:20 MSG

Samantha needed money. She had time to add a part-time job to her busy schedule, and she heard from a friend about a company that was paying people to sell energy drinks from home in their spare time. That sounded good to her! She'd rather not have to go into work anywhere if she could do everything from home. So she scrounged up some money and bought the expensive start-up kit. She followed all of the instructions, and soon, boxes and boxes of energy drinks showed up at her door. Samantha was so excited. She started tallying how much money she would have if she sold every box. She'd be rich by the end of the month!

She started texting and emailing everyone in her contact list. Weird. No one was getting back to her. So she tried again. Nothing. Huh. Not one person wanted to buy a box of energy drinks from her. Not even her parents! By the end of the month, Samantha had no money and a garage full of warm energy drinks. Talk about regrets! This is a sad but true story. And stories like this have been happening for ages.

In old movies, this was called being a "snake-oil salesman." A con man would put some liquid in a jar and tell people it could cure whatever ailment they had. They would drive their wagons full of the product through town, and people who were in pain would buy it. Then the salesmen would leave town before the buyers found out that it didn't actually work.

Get-rich quick schemes are always out there, so be aware! They take many forms, but basically someone at the very top is getting rich off of someone at the very bottom buying their useless product. (They don't call it a pyramid scheme for nothin'!) As they say, if something sounds too good to be true, it usually is. That's a lesson you can take to the bank.

Have you ever been ripped off? It feels crummy, doesn't it?

The Bible tells us that "committed and persistent work" is what pays off. If you want to make good, honest money, you have to work hard at something to earn a fair wage. Be on the lookout for "easy money" as you get older. That should be a red flag to pay attention to. It's better to do things God's way and avoid a garage full of regret!

Lord, please help me to pay attention to the internal warning system You've given me. Help me to be wise when it comes to work and money. Give me the desire to do good, honest work that pleases You.

THE CLASS CLOWN

*Show respect for all people [treat them honorably], love
the brotherhood [of believers], fear God, honor the king.*
1 PETER 2:17 AMP

Terry was clever and funny. She could make people laugh and
crack a good joke that had her friends crying with tears of silli-
ness. She was a fun friend. But she needed to mature a bit in
this area. Sometimes she used humor in inappropriate ways. She
had a hard time being serious. She sometimes made jokes out
of the teacher's lecture during class. She'd whisper funnies to
her friends during church. She could make anything into a joke.

A kind and loving teacher took her aside and told her that
her humor was out of place in the classroom during teaching.
The teacher didn't shame her or try to get her to feel bad about
herself. She wanted Terry to know that joking around and being
joyful and clever can be a good thing, as long as it's during
appropriate times.

Ecclesiastes 3:1, 4 (NIV) says, "There is a time for everything,
and a season for every activity under the heavens. . .a time to
weep and a time to laugh, a time to mourn and a time to dance."

Terry listened to that kind and loving teacher. She learned to
be respectful of others and to think before she spoke or made
a joke. If something struck her as funny during the teacher's
lecture, she'd wait until lunch to share: "Remember when Mrs.
Smith said that? I thought it was so funny because. . ."

Laughter is literally good medicine. Proverbs 17:22 (NIV)

says, "A cheerful heart is good medicine, but a crushed spirit dries up the bones." And many studies have been conducted on how laughter and a joyful spirit can bring stress levels down. Laughter is healing for your body and good for the soul.

And so is respect. If you have something funny to say, make sure it's not something you'll regret later. There is a time and a place for jokes. And a joke should be for all the listeners, not an inside joke that makes some people feel left out when you tell it. And when you tell a joke, make sure you're not making fun of other people or putting others down just for a laugh.

Humor that honors God is the kind that you won't regret.

Lord Jesus, thank You for humor and laughter. I know You created it to bring us joy and to decrease stress. Help me to use humor wisely in my life. Show me how to respect others when I'm trying to be funny.

DO THE WORK GOD GAVE YOU

*"I have glorified You [down here] on the earth by
completing the work that You gave Me to do. . . . Just as
You commissioned and sent Me into the world, I also have
commissioned and sent them (believers) into the world."*

JOHN 17:4, 18 AMP

God designed you with special gifts and abilities. And He sent you to earth at this point in time on purpose, for a purpose. Hard to believe? Check it out:

* " 'For I know the plans I have for you,' declares the LORD, 'plans to prosper you and not to harm you, plans to give you hope and a future' " (Jeremiah 29:11 NIV).

* "The LORD will fulfill his purpose for me; your steadfast love, O LORD, endures forever. Do not forsake the work of your hands" (Psalm 138:8 ESV).

* "When all has been heard, the end of the matter is: fear God [worship Him with awe-filled reverence, knowing that He is almighty God] and keep His commandments, for this applies to every person" (Ecclesiastes 12:13 AMP).

* We know that God causes everything to work together for the good of those who love God and are called according to his purpose for them" (Romans 8:28 NLT).

In the book of Jeremiah, God says, "I knew you before I formed you in your mother's womb" (1:5 NLT). And if that's not enough, Psalm 139:1–5 (NLT) will blow your mind! "O LORD, you have examined my heart and know everything about me. You know when I sit down or stand up. You know my thoughts even when I'm far away. You see me when I travel and when I rest at home. You know everything I do. You know what I am going to say even before I say it, LORD. You go before me and follow me. You place your hand of blessing on my head."

God knows everything about you, and He loves you deeply. Even with all your regrets and mistakes. He loves you so much that He sent His Son to die for you and complete the work the Father gave Him. God has important plans and purposes for your life too. And you don't want to miss them!

So, how do you find out what your special purpose and mission is? Keep following Jesus. When Jesus called James and John to come follow Him and become His disciples, they were fishermen. They were doing the work God gave them. Little did they know that they were about to change the whole world.

As you follow Jesus, He will reveal more and more of Himself and His purpose for you, day by day. It's going to be a great adventure!

Lord, I don't want to miss what You have for me. I'm thankful to be on this journey with You. Fill me with Your love and purpose.

CORN ON THE COB

"But whoever drinks the water that I give him will never be thirsty again. But the water that I give him will become in him a spring of water [satisfying his thirst for God] welling up [continually flowing, bubbling within him] to eternal life."

JOHN 4:14 AMP

In our giant garden, everything is an experiment. When we moved to this area, I didn't know very much about gardening. I had to read lots of tutorials and watch a lot of videos to know what and how to plant such a massive area. Thankfully, the lovely people who lived here before us were gardeners. They spent years developing fertile soil. They also tapped into the sprinkler system so that the garden would get watered regularly. They really set us up for success.

This year, we decided to plant sweet corn. I read articles specifically about planting sweet corn. I even planted some companion plants that would help the sweet corn resist disease and bugs. The goal was that the cornstalks would grow to "knee high by the fourth of July." We had to plant a little bit late because of the cool weather here, but by the time the fireworks were going off all over the state, my little stalks of corn had grown to my knees.

By mid-August, I began noticing that many gardens around my area had rows of sweet corn that were puny. The stalks were thin and spindly. They didn't look healthy at all. Our summer had been dry, so I realized that gardens not connected to a steady water source were suffering. A little garden-hose watering here and there just wasn't going to cut it in our drought.

Our corn was tall and lush and full in comparison. Our sprinkler system saved my corn. During the dry spells, our corn still had a steady source of water. And I was reminded that we can learn a lot about Jesus from the garden!

Like sweet corn, our bodies were designed to need water—not just to quench our thirst but to quench our hearts. We were designed to need living water from Jesus Himself. A little bit of Jesus here and there, like the occasional watering from a garden hose, just isn't going to cut it. Your spiritual life will end up puny and bitter. But if you're regularly connected to the source of life Himself, your spiritual life will be vibrant and healthy and sweet.

Jesus, I need Your constant life-giving water in my heart. When I'm thirsty for love and acceptance, help me to come to You—and not to social media or lesser things—to get those needs met.

LISTENING TO GOD

"My sheep listen to my voice;
I know them, and they follow me."
John 10:27 NIV

Many "celebrity Christians" have deconstructed their faith over the past few years. They made names for themselves as Bible-believing Christians and then decided they didn't believe God's way anymore. And they did it very publicly. Authors, musicians, and pastors just decided they no longer believed in the God of the Bible. The sad thing is that many Christians who had put those celebrities on pedestals then followed them right over a cliff.

Sheep do that. For real! A few years back there was a news story about one sheep in the country of Turkey who jumped over a cliff. Sheep follow their leaders. Fifteen hundred other sheep watched this one sheep jump over the cliff, and can you guess what they did? They jumped too!

That's why it's so important for us to be listening to and following after God's voice. The Bible has a lot to say about hearing from God:

* "Call to me and I will answer you and tell you great and unsearchable things you do not know" (Jeremiah 33:3 NIV).

* "But Jesus replied, 'It is written and forever remains written, "Man shall not live by bread alone, but by every word that comes out of the mouth of God" ' " (Matthew 4:4 AMP).

* "All Scripture is inspired by God and is useful to teach us what is true and to make us realize what is wrong in our lives. It corrects us when we are wrong and teaches us to do what is right" (2 Timothy 3:16 NLT).

* "For He whom God has sent speaks the words of God [proclaiming the Father's own message]; for God gives the [gift of the] Spirit without measure [generously and boundlessly]!" (John 3:34 AMP).

* "The heavens are telling of the glory of God; and the expanse [of heaven] is declaring the work of His hands" (Psalm 19:1 AMP).

* "Let the word of Christ dwell in you richly, teaching and admonishing one another in all wisdom, singing psalms and hymns and spiritual songs, with thankfulness in your hearts to God" (Colossians 3:16 ESV).

* "You search the Scriptures because you think they give you eternal life. But the Scriptures point to me! Yet you refuse to come to me to receive this life" (John 5:39–40 NLT).

Through the power of the Holy Spirit, you can hear from God in many ways—through creation, through His Word, through other people God sends you, through music and songs. Jesus says that we can know His voice and follow after Him.

Lord, help me learn to listen for and know Your voice in my life. If I'm going to be a sheep, I want to be in Your pasture only.

CATS AND POISON IVY

Do what is good and run from evil so that you
may live! Then the LORD God of Heaven's Armies
will be your helper, just as you have claimed.
AMOS 5:14 NLT

We have two cats, Cricket and Louie. We brought Cricket home when he was only a couple of months old. When he got older, we let him come and go as he pleased. But instead of catching field mice, he was mostly interested in visiting the cat across the street.

We live out in the country, but our road is busy. Cars fly past our house on their way into town. And Cricket would just meander across the road to see his friend. My daughter loves Cricket very much, and she was worried that he would get hit. So we decided to build Cricket a special "catio"—cat patio—in our woods.

We had to clear out the area because it was full of vines and other foliage. My husband saw some poison ivy growing up the trees. He put on gloves and was very careful not to touch it. But poison ivy is insidious. It looks harmless enough but is actually toxic.

After a day of removing the foliage without any adverse reaction, my husband thought he'd protected himself well enough and forgot about it. But it turns out that, even without the green plant on them, the vines of poison ivy are toxic too. And he'd been building the walls of the catio all over those vines.

By midweek he was covered in a blistering and oozing rash all over his body. He had to go to the doctor for special medicine to get the rash to clear up. Talk about regret!

The enemy comes at us like this a lot. Something looks nice enough—a new friend, a club at school, an activity, an app, a video—but then you get into it, and something doesn't seem right. Before you know it, you're surrounded by something poisonous to your heart and mind.

When you notice that is happening, run! Run like poison ivy is everywhere. Turn back to Jesus and let Him help you find the way out (1 Corinthians 10:13). He is with you always, and He will help before you end up in regret.

Lord Jesus, help me to run away from evil as soon as I realize it for what it really is. Protect my heart and mind. Help me pay attention to those warning signals You give me. When my body starts building a defense and my heart starts pounding, show me the way back to You.

REGRETS WITH CRICKET

*No discipline is enjoyable while it is happening—
it's painful! But afterward there will be a peaceful harvest
of right living for those who are trained in this way.*
HEBREWS 12:11 NLT

Cricket was supposed to be a barn cat. We wanted him to catch mice since we are surrounded by cornfields where they live and they tend to take day excursions to our house. But Cricket wasn't interested in real mice. He just liked to play with stuffed mice that tasted of catnip like we gave him when he was a baby. After he got older, he got into a bad fight with a ground squirrel and the little ground squirrel won. Cricket wasn't expecting the animal to actually fight back! Cricket's face was scratched and bloody. Poor kitty. Cricket just wasn't interested in real outdoor cat activities (except visiting that friend of his across the street!). He liked to eat a lot too and was getting quite fat. Apparently, we spoiled him for the outside world of a cat.

It seems that Cricket will never be a good mouser. Now he spends most of his day lounging in his spacious catio (safe from the ground squirrels!), watching little Louie play and enjoying regular visits from his people on his favorite bench. And the mice aren't scared at all. In fact, they're probably laughing at us!

Bad habits are hard to break. We started some bad habits with Cricket, and we'd completely spoiled him. We fed him too much. We gave him too many mouse toys. He was turning into a black-and-white version of that fat orange cat from the cartoons!

Are you struggling with a bad habit? Maybe eating too much sugar or spending too much time on screens? Unlike Cricket, you have a choice and the power of the Holy Spirit at work in you to make good and necessary changes.

Romans 8:11 (NLT) says, "The Spirit of God, who raised Jesus from the dead, lives in you. And just as God raised Christ Jesus from the dead, he will give life to your mortal bodies by this same Spirit living within you."

How awesome is that? You don't have to live in defeat. If God is calling you to be healthy in an area, you can. If you want to beat a bad habit, He will help. His Spirit is alive in you—the same Spirit who raised Jesus from the dead (Ephesians 1:19–20).

Awesome resurrection power from God is available to you in every moment. With God's help, you can kick your bad habits out of your life for good.

Wow, Lord! I'm learning some incredible stuff about Your power at work in my heart and in my life! I'm ready to cooperate as You change me from the inside out.

LOVING AND LETTING GO

I know the LORD is always with me. I will not
be shaken, for he is right beside me.
PSALM 16:8 NLT

Life is full of hellos and goodbyes. We've told our kids this for years. We've had lots of moves across town and across country. We've said hello and goodbye to many friends and family members. We've had relationships that were broken. We've had people pass away that we loved deeply. There were good relationships and happy memories and also many regrets as we learned from our mistakes and grew deeper in our relationships with God.

One thing we learned along the way is that sometimes the most loving thing to do for a person is to let them go. As we got healthier on the inside and repented of our own toxic and sinful ways, God started opening our eyes to some toxic relationships that we had allowed to continue for too long.

Psalm 101:3–6 (AMP) says, "I will set no worthless or wicked thing before my eyes. I hate the practice of those who fall away [from the right path]; it will not grasp hold of me. A perverse heart shall depart from me; I will not tolerate evil. Whoever secretly slanders his neighbor, him I will silence; the one who has a haughty look and a proud (arrogant) heart I will not tolerate. My eyes will be on the faithful (honorable) of the land, that they may dwell with me."

Walking away from relationships marked by gossip and pride is a hard thing to do. Especially when it's with people you've been close to for many years. Maybe it's a friendship you've had since kindergarten or a neighbor or a boyfriend or a family member.

If God is asking you to walk away from a relationship, He will confirm that in you over and over. As you pray, the Holy Spirit will prompt your heart that it's the right thing to do. You might hear it again at church from a pastor or youth leader. You might be encouraged through a song on the radio. God will be clear with you if this is something He wants you to do. And then He will give you the courage and strength to do the loving thing for yourself and for the other person.

It might feel lonely at first, but be encouraged: "The LORD himself watches over you! The LORD stands beside you as your protective shade" (Psalm 121:5 NLT).

And "May the grace of the Lord Jesus Christ, the love of God, and the fellowship of the Holy Spirit be with you all" (2 Corinthians 13:14 NLT).

Lord, I need Your reassurance and Your comfort as I walk away from unhealthy relationships. Thank You for watching over me and giving me courage to do the loving thing.

CONVERSATIONS I REGRET

May these words of my mouth and this meditation of my heart be pleasing in your sight, Lord, my Rock and my Redeemer.
PSALM 19:14 NIV

Tiffani went out to coffee with her friend. They loved their coffee dates. Sometimes hours would pass as they would talk about everything. Usually, their conversations were about faith and family, and they were encouraging and uplifting. But one day, Tiffani got home and felt convicted by God that she'd said too much and the wrong thing about something. She sent her friend a text, apologizing and asking for forgiveness for her part of the conversation. She also asked God to help her steer clear of conversations that didn't honor Him in the future.

God's Word has a lot to tell us about our words! Check out these verses:

* "Death and life are in the power of the tongue, and those who love it and indulge it will eat its fruit and bear the consequences of their words" (Proverbs 18:21 AMP).

* "Understand this, my dear brothers and sisters: You must all be quick to listen, slow to speak, and slow to get angry" (James 1:19 NLT).

* "But now you must also rid yourselves of all such things as these: anger, rage, malice, slander, and filthy language from your lips" (Colossians 3:8 NIV).

* "Do not let any unwholesome talk come out of your mouths, but only what is helpful for building others up according to their needs, that it may benefit those who listen" (Ephesians 4:29 NIV).

* "Let your speech at all times be gracious and pleasant, seasoned with salt, so that you will know how to answer each one [who questions you]" (Colossians 4:6 AMP).

* "He who guards his mouth and his tongue guards himself from troubles" (Proverbs 21:23 AMP).

* "And whatever you do or say, do it as a representative of the Lord Jesus, giving thanks through him to God the Father" (Colossians 3:17 NLT).

Words can heal and words can curse. Words can bring life and words can tear down. Our words have power.

If you struggle with your words, it's time to have a long talk with Jesus. He wants to help you mature in this area.

Lord Jesus, I want to talk about good and encouraging things that honor You. I repent of not watching my words carefully in the past. I repent of talking badly about people and issues. Help me think before I speak instead of blurting out everything I'm thinking and feeling. Help me to grow up in this area. Thank You, Jesus!

VOLLEYBALL TOURNAMENTS AND TESTS

*All Scripture is God-breathed and is useful for
teaching, rebuking, correcting and training in
righteousness, so that the servant of God may be
thoroughly equipped for every good work.*
2 TIMOTHY 3:16–17 NIV

Jessa's first volleyball game of the year was a tournament. A year had gone by since her last tournament, and we had largely forgotten many of the details. We drove over two hours to get there. We packed food and water. But by midmorning, we realized we had forgotten many necessary things. The day was long with six games expected. There were short breaks in between games. We were there from 8:00 in the morning until after 7:00 p.m. We ran out of food and water early. It ended up being a very expensive day, running here and there to buy things we had forgotten.

Many people regret being unprepared. Unprepared for a test. Unprepared for a storm. Unprepared for a job interview. Have you ever been given a test and when you looked at the questions you realized you didn't know very many of the answers? That can be terrifying!

Thankfully, you don't have to worry about being unprepared for life with Jesus. Why? Because God is in the equipping business.

Today's verse reminds us that God has given us His Word so that His followers can be ready for anything. Spending time in God's Word every day and learning to listen for His voice will prepare and equip you for everything that's coming your way in this life and in the next.

Hebrews 13:21 (NLT) says, "May [God] equip you with all you need for doing his will. May he produce in you, through the power of Jesus Christ, every good thing that is pleasing to him. All glory to him forever and ever! Amen."

So this means that He not only equips you for everything He calls you to do but He also empowers you to do it! That's like taking an open-book test and having the teacher right there with you helping you with every answer. Wouldn't it be great if more tests were like that?

Through the power of Jesus Christ, God is producing every good thing in you. You don't have to worry about not being a good enough Christian or working overtime to prove yourself to God and others. That gets exhausting. Let God do the work in you. Trust His mighty power and His Word. All you have to do is stay connected to Him and cooperate with the process.

Lord, I sometimes struggle with trying to prove myself. It does get exhausting. Please change my heart and mind on this. Help me trust that You want to do the powerful work in me. Help me get into Your Word and stay close to You as You do the transforming work.

HEART RENOVATION

Heal me, O LORD, and I will be healed; save me
and I will be saved, for You are my praise.
JEREMIAH 17:14 AMP

There used to be a show on TV called *Extreme Makeover: Home Edition.* The creators, along with the help of neighbors and construction crews, would completely renovate a house for a family in need. It was fun to watch a house in disrepair turn into a beautiful home in just one week.

Sadly, another video made after only a few short years showed that quite a few of those families had lost their renovated homes. Some fell into more financial hardship. Others couldn't overcome the trauma of their past, and it continued.

An ancient idiom says, "Wherever you go, there you are." Basically, it means that unless you find and repair what's broken in your life, you take that brokenness into a new space. The space has changed, but you haven't. "Wherever you go, there you are."

And that can happen to any of us. It's sad that the families on *Extreme Makeover* had such a public display of their hardship and the loss of their updated homes. We don't know what's going on behind the scenes in anyone's family, and so we have no place judging and criticizing what we don't understand. But we can learn something from this.

Many people run from one bad situation to the next. They leave a toxic relationship only to find the same type of guy with a different face. They move to a new town or state to escape bad situations and relationships from their past only to find themselves in very similar situations and relationships. Why does this keep happening? Often, it's because the brokenness inside them that is attracting these situations and relationships has never been fixed. Their location has changed, but their heart hasn't.

If you find yourself going through difficult situations over and over again, it's time to take a deep dive into your heart to see what needs healing in there.

Here are three things to ask Jesus in this situation: highlight, heal, and help. Use this scripture as your guide: "Search me, O God, and know my heart; test me and know my anxious thoughts. Point out anything in me that offends you, and lead me along the path of everlasting life" (Psalm 139:23–24 NLT).

Ask God to highlight anything in you that is causing the brokenness. Maybe it's a childhood trauma, hard feelings inside, or unconfessed sin. Ask Him to heal the broken places. Then ask Him for help to change. There is a healthy way forward!

Lord, would You do a renovation in my heart?
Show me anything in me that is out of alignment.
Heal the places in me that are broken. And help me
to move forward in healthy ways. Thank You, Jesus!

MOLD AND MESSES

After you have suffered for a little while, the God
of all grace [who imparts His blessing and favor],
who called you to His own eternal glory in Christ,
will Himself complete, confirm, strengthen, and
establish you [making you what you ought to be].
1 PETER 5:10 AMP

We have a sunroom that surrounds two sides of our house around back. It has two levels. The main floor has an outdoor couch and chairs, and then three steps down, there is a smaller floor with a dining table. The entire thing is full of windows. There have been times when we've forgotten to shut the windows during a rainstorm and the floor has gotten wet. Or children have walked through that area from the backyard, soaking wet from playing in the water.

Over the summer, we noticed two spots in the floor that were getting a little wonky. We'd sink a little when we stepped on those areas. We didn't think much about it. But then those spots got bigger, and it felt like we might break right through the floor. We needed to see what was going on underneath.

We pulled up the vinyl flooring and found mold and wood rot. We had to get rid of all the damaged wood, clean up the mess, and put down a new floor. We definitely regretted letting water sit on that floor! What a mess it caused, and much of it was our fault.

Relationships can get messy too. A little recurring problem

that seems insignificant at the time can turn into something big before you know it. And sometimes you're the one who causes the mess! You may start to feel like you don't know what to do or even where to begin to clean it up.

Thankfully, Jesus doesn't just stand at the door and watch us squirm. One pastor said that He's the kind of friend who shows up at your door and brings a broom. The Bible tells us that the God of all grace will Himself "complete, confirm, strengthen, and establish you." He's the one who will help you make things right and make you what you ought to be. The New Living Translation says, "He will restore, support, and strengthen you, and he will place you on a firm foundation."

Your part is to trust Him and let Him in the door.

If you're in the middle of a relationship mess, open up the door and let Jesus come in with the broom. Sometimes the mess you make is too big for you to try and clean up alone. Only God can see all sides of a situation. Let Him help.

Lord, I've made a mess of things, and I'm not sure what to do. Please help me! Show me what to do next.

CARL AND JOSEPH

"As for you, you meant evil against me, but God meant it for good, to bring it about that many people should be kept alive, as they are today."
Genesis 50:20 esv

Carl was a good kid, but he surrounded himself with some troublemakers as he was growing up. He got himself into all kinds of trouble because of that. Carl was a talented artist, but instead of using his talent for good, he would tag public places with graffiti.

Carl grew up and found himself with a similar group of friends. But one of those friends started going to church, and he invited Carl. Carl thought he'd give it a try and ended up going to a small group where he encountered the living God. He gave his life to Jesus, and his life started turning around. Soon, Carl's church started finding out about his amazing art skills. They were planning an upcoming series that needed some artwork painted on a brick wall. Carl was the guy to do it! He used his skills to glorify God.

God is in the habit of taking bad situations and turning them around for good. Toward the end of the book of Genesis in the Bible, we learn about Joseph and his brothers. Joseph's brothers were jealous of him, and they sold him into slavery. They lied to their dad and made it look like Joseph had been killed. Years later, Joseph ended up saving his brothers from famine as he rose to power in Egypt. The book of Genesis ends with Joseph forgiving his brothers. He realized that God intended for him to be brought to Egypt so that he could save the lives of many. And even though his brothers had meant evil against him, God used it for good.

God can turn situations and relationships and people around and change them in extraordinary ways. Ephesians 3:20–21 (NIV) says, "Now to him who is able to do immeasurably more than all we ask or imagine, according to his power that is at work within us, to him be glory in the church and in Christ Jesus throughout all generations, for ever and ever! Amen."

Don't despair. If you have a friend who is far from God, remember Carl and his life. If you have a relationship that is severed because of sin against you, remember Joseph. God is able to do way more than you can ever ask or imagine! Trust Him.

God, I believe that You can do more than I could ever imagine. I pray for the people and situations in my life that need Your miraculous creativity and healing touch. I trust that You can turn everything around into something good.

PARTIES AND FORGIVENESS

*So whoever knows the right thing to do
and fails to do it, for him it is sin.*
JAMES 4:17 ESV

Ivy loved having get-togethers at her house. She had a big home with a finished basement and a pool in the backyard. She liked to invite her friends over for swimming parties, tea parties, movie nights, and more. It was super fun, and her friends loved coming over. But what Ivy didn't like was cleaning before the party and cleaning up after the party. Her mom told her that she was willing to allow Ivy to have parties as long as she helped with all the cleaning. At her last gathering, she was sluggish when it came time to get things ready for the party. And afterward, she was too tired to help at all. She went to bed and left the cleaning for her mom and dad. The next day, she had forgotten all about it.

A month went by, and Ivy's friends were asking if they could come over and swim. They were ready for another party. So Ivy planned a party with her friends without asking. A few days before the party, she mentioned the plan to her mom, who had always said yes before. But this time was different. Ivy's mom reminded her how she had left the mess for her parents to clean up last time, and her consequence was to cancel the party. Ivy was bummed. So were her friends.

Being responsible and keeping your word are big parts of maturing. Ivy had some repair work to do here. She apologized to her parents for leaving them with all the cleaning after she had committed to help. She apologized to her friends for being irresponsible the last time they came over and for not checking with her mom before she planned the party. Ivy felt very embarrassed over the whole thing.

The good news is that she had a great set of friends who forgave her for her mistakes, her parents gave her grace and allowed her to plan a future party to earn back their trust, and God forgave her too.

Ephesians 4:32 (NIV) says, "Be kind and compassionate to one another, forgiving each other, just as in Christ God forgave you." Ivy got to experience that verse personally.

If you've made a mistake that involves several people, go to them and make it right. It might be embarrassing and difficult, but God is with you. He doesn't want you to carry sin and regret around, bringing you down. He wants you to be free.

Lord, thanks so much for Your grace as I'm growing up and learning to be more responsible and faithful. Thank You for Your compassion, Your forgiveness, and Your great love for me!

BOUNDARIES AT THE YOUTH RETREAT

Carry each other's burdens, and in this way you will fulfill the law of Christ. If anyone thinks they are something when they are not, they deceive themselves. Each one should test their own actions. Then they can take pride in themselves alone, without comparing themselves to someone else, for each one should carry their own load.

GALATIANS 6:2–5 NIV

Ella went with her youth group on a ski trip. She has some digestive issues, so she has to be very careful about what she eats or she'll end up with a bad stomachache. She takes several supplements to help with her digestion. One day into the trip, she was doing fine. But then her friends next to her were eating food she felt like she couldn't resist. She gave in and ate a lot of junk food. She also forgot to take her supplements. Then she had to get on a bus for the ride home. She ate more junk food that she had stashed in her backpack. It was there. She was hungry. So she ate it. But then, her stomach started protesting for Ella's lack of care over the weekend. By the time the bus pulled into the church parking lot, she could barely move, her stomach hurt so bad. She wouldn't forget this life lesson for a long time!

Doing the right thing when everyone around you is doing something tempting can be difficult. Ella was in a hard situation. Her friends weren't doing anything wrong; she just knew it wasn't good for her personally. She needed to develop some good boundaries. Ella learned that she needed to set the timer on her phone to remind herself to take her supplements when she was away from home. She also confided in a few close friends that it was difficult for her to stay away from junk food when everyone else was eating it. They were kind and loving and said they would help her next time by eating healthier or going for a walk with her when everyone else broke into the junk food. Ella took responsibility for herself and also asked for help.

The Amplified Bible translates today's verse like this: "Carry one another's burdens and in this way you will fulfill the requirements of the law of Christ [that is, the law of Christian love]." Helping someone else carry their burden is loving. It is also loving to have good and healthy boundaries, for each person is responsible to carry their own load and responsibilities.

Lord, thank You for helping me know what is mine to carry and when I should ask for help. I want to develop good and healthy boundaries with Your help.

SOWING AND REAPING IN RELATIONSHIPS

*Remember this—a farmer who plants only a
few seeds will get a small crop. But the one who
plants generously will get a generous crop.*
2 CORINTHIANS 9:6 NLT

Michelle was in a painful relationship. She loved her friend and wanted to help her, but she felt like the entire relationship revolved around helping her friend get out of one crisis and then another. Over and over again. There was a lot of drama. Michelle was torn because her friend was a fairly new Christian. She wanted to show her friend the love of Jesus, but she also felt like something was wrong in their friendship.

Michelle went to see a wise and older Christian mentor she knew who loved Jesus. She shared with her mentor what was happening, and her mentor gave her some very good advice. The mentor told her, "You are getting in the way of the law of sowing and reaping."

Her mentor explained that the Bible talks about reaping what you sow. Galatians 6:7 (ESV) says, "Do not be deceived: God is not mocked, for whatever one sows, that will he also reap."

If you plant corn in a garden, you're going to grow corn. Likewise, if you plant sin and toxicity in your life, you're going to grow more sin and more toxicity.

Michelle began to see that her friend did not have good

boundaries. She relied on Michelle too much to help her out of her problems. Her friend continued to plant sin in her life, and Michelle was getting in the way of the reaping, trying to rescue her. Michelle's friend needed to experience the consequences of her poor choices and seek Jesus as her rescuer instead.

Jesus said to love your neighbor as yourself (Matthew 22:39). Michelle had tried to be loving to her friend, but she wasn't being very loving to herself by exhausting herself physically, emotionally, and spiritually when she was in rescue mode for her friend.

Michelle began to pray for her friend instead of trying to rescue her. Honestly, Michelle's friend didn't like it much when Michelle stopped helping her out of her problems. But Michelle knew it was the right and most loving choice she could make—for her friend and for herself.

Soon Michelle began to reap what she was sowing too. She planted peace, freedom, and love generously. And she began to reap more peace, more freedom, and more love. She became a much healthier and more loving person after she set good boundaries in her life and released her friend into the care of Jesus.

Lord, as I plant love and peace generously in my heart, please help it grow abundantly. Show me how to love others and care for myself well too.

LATE-NIGHT ICE CREAM

*The prudent see danger and take refuge, but the
simple keep going and pay the penalty.*
PROVERBS 22:3 NIV

Natalie and her mom were watching videos on a food blog right before bed. The camera zoomed in on a hot fudge brownie sundae that looked amazing. Natalie and her mom had the sudden urge to go get ice cream! So they did. The ice cream shop nearby was open for another half hour, and off they went. Natalie got a milkshake, and her mom got a hot fudge sundae. The first few bites were delicious. Then they got about halfway through their treats, realized how late it actually was, and wondered what they were thinking! They were never going to be able to sleep well with all that sugar in their bodies. So they stayed up later than usual. Both mom and daughter had a hard time sleeping and woke up groggy the next day. They thought ice cream was a good idea in the moment, but they paid for it later. They decided together that they would no longer be watching food blogs right before bed. Maybe right after lunch would be a better idea!

Learning from our mistakes is a sign of maturity. Proverbs 1:5 (NIV) says, "Let the wise listen and add to their learning, and let the discerning get guidance."

Everyone makes mistakes; it's what you do after them that matters. If you've done something you regret—big or little—there is a way to move forward in a healthy way.

It's important to try again after messing up. Don't let fear hold you back. Tomorrow will be a new day without any screwups in it yet. You can try again. Wise people learn from their messes, and they make plans to do things differently in the future. Natalie and her mom learned not to watch shows about sugary food right before bed.

Proverbs 24:16 (NLT) says, "The godly may trip seven times, but they will get up again. But one disaster is enough to over-throw the wicked." *The Message* says it this way: "No matter how many times you trip them up, God-loyal people don't stay down long; soon they're up on their feet, while the wicked end up flat on their faces."

Lord, thanks for giving me the opportunity to try again. Help me learn from my mistakes, big and small. Thank You that I don't have to be defeated by my failures. You are with me, teaching me and helping me get back up again.

HORSE AND RIDER

When I am afraid, I put my trust in you.
PSALM 56:3 NIV

Heidi was a champion equestrian in high school. She had two beautiful horses, and her friend Kelly wanted to come over to ride. It was a beautiful summer day, perfect for a short ride with her friend. Heidi's dad had told her many times not to saddle her horse without him there. But he was at work, and Heidi knew what she was doing. She'd done it many times. She saddled up her horse and allowed Kelly to take a short ride.

Kelly was having a ton of fun. She was not an experienced rider at all, but she got on and began to walk the horse around the pasture. Soon they were up to a trot and then a full canter. This was too fast for Kelly. They went around a corner, and the saddle began to shift. Before she knew it, Kelly was on the ground with a hurt shoulder. Heidi could saddle a horse well enough for herself, but Kelly was bigger and taller than Heidi. The saddle hadn't been tightened securely enough for Kelly.

Of course Heidi got in trouble with her dad, and Kelly was left with a wounded shoulder that took weeks to heal. All because they didn't obey Heidi's dad's instructions. Sadly, Kelly was afraid of horses after that and decided never to get on a horse again. She missed out on many adventures due to her fear.

Facing your fears is never an easy thing. The Bible has a lot to say to us to help us overcome fear in any situation. Take a look:

* "Be strong and courageous. Do not be afraid or terrified because of them, for the LORD your God goes with you; he will never leave you nor forsake you" (Deuteronomy 31:6 NIV).

* "Give all your worries and cares to God, for he cares about you" (1 Peter 5:7 NLT).

* "Though a mighty army surrounds me, my heart will not be afraid. Even if I am attacked, I will remain confident" (Psalm 27:3 NLT).

* "What is the price of two sparrows—one copper coin? But not a single sparrow can fall to the ground without your Father knowing it. And the very hairs on your head are all numbered. So don't be afraid; you are more valuable to God than a whole flock of sparrows" (Matthew 10:29–31 NLT).

If you have a fear that needs facing, take it to Jesus. Be encouraged that He sees you and He cares. He is gentle with you and will not force you into anything against your will. You can trust Him to take care of you as you give up your fears into His mighty and loving hands.

Lord, I don't want to miss out on great adventures because I'm afraid. Help me to trust You more.

SURPRISED TO BE LOVED

He reached down from on high and took hold of me; he drew me out of deep waters. He rescued me from my powerful enemy, from my foes, who were too strong for me. They confronted me in the day of my disaster, but the LORD was my support. He brought me out into a spacious place; he rescued me because he delighted in me.

PSALM 18:16–19 NIV

Remember Michelle? She's the one who was learning how to have good boundaries with herself and others. In that process, she realized that she had been believing some lies about herself and God.

Due to some trauma in her past, Michelle had a hard time believing she was loved. Though she honored God and sought to please Him, she had a deep belief that God was always disappointed in her. That she was never doing enough to make Him happy.

As Michelle started pursuing health in her heart, mind, and body, the Holy Spirit began revealing God's truth to her. She had heard John 3:16 (NIV) most of her life: "For God so loved the world that he gave his one and only Son." But she had a hard time putting her name into that sentence. It seemed like it was for everyone else she was taught to share that with and not herself.

But God kept pursuing Michelle's heart. He really wanted her to know how loved she was. Zephaniah 3:17 (NLT) says, "For the LORD your God is living among you. He is a mighty savior. He will take delight in you with gladness. With his love, he will calm all your fears. He will rejoice over you with joyful songs."

Michelle began waking up with worship songs in her heart and mind. She began listening for the voice of God in her life. She came across today's verse in *The Message*, and it stunned her: "But me he caught—reached all the way from sky to sea; he pulled me out of that ocean of hate, that enemy chaos, the void in which I was drowning. They hit me when I was down, but GOD stuck by me. He stood me up on a wide-open field; I stood there saved—surprised to be loved!"

That's exactly how she felt! God reached out and saved Michelle from drowning in a sea of doubt, discouragement, and unprocessed trauma. God was with her through it all, speaking love and truth over her. What a delight and surprise to find out that she was actually loved!

Because of Jesus and His completed work for her, God was not disappointed in Michelle—He was delighted! The same is true for you.

You are loved with an everlasting love that doesn't change due to circumstances or feelings (Jeremiah 31:3).

Thank You, Father, for Your powerful, unfailing, everlasting, always-and-forever love for me!

OLLIE AND DAISY

Ollie and Daisy are very different. Ollie is very outgoing and playful. Daisy is shy and sneaky. Both are loving and smart. Ollie joyfully licks strangers, and Daisy barks and growls at them. Did I mention Ollie and Daisy are dogs?

Ollie goes to obedience class because he loses his mind around other dogs. He is an Australian shepherd, so he just wants to herd everyone into a circle. That's all. What's all the fuss about? He doesn't understand why he can't be noisy around other animals. He was bred to do that.

Daisy, on the other hand, isn't bothered by animals, but she does not like strangers. At first, we thought we should probably take her to obedience class too so that she would do better around new people. But she obeys us pretty well already, and we decided we might regret that decision. You see, Daisy is a very good watchdog.

Ollie and Daisy spend most of their day outside. They sleep in the barn, and they have the full run of the fenced-in woods, right next to the catio. While Ollie would go home with anyone who even faintly hinted of bacon, Daisy alerts us to intruders right away. If anyone is on our property, Daisy knows about it and tells us. We decided we liked that alert system and didn't want to train it out of her.

You have a built-in alert system like that too. The Holy Spirit inside you is there to teach you and guide you. When you're about to do something you know is wrong, you've felt your heart beat fast in your chest, right? That's your internal warning system at work. That's the Holy Spirit telling you to pay attention and look for the way out that Jesus promises in 1 Corinthians 10:13.

But what happens if you keep ignoring that internal warning system? You'll start hearing it less and less when you need it most, essentially "training" it out of yourself until you can hardly hear the alert at all.

Galatians 5:25 (AMP) says, "If we [claim to] live by the [Holy] Spirit, we must also walk by the Spirit [with personal integrity, godly character, and moral courage—our conduct empowered by the Holy Spirit]."

As you live and walk by the Holy Spirit, pay attention to what He is telling you. Listen as He leads and guides you into the paths that He has for you.

Lord, thank You for working in my heart and for speaking to me. Help me to be sensitive to what You're saying. Let me hear You and obey.

SELFISHNESS AND PINCHED TOES

Don't be selfish; don't try to impress others.
Be humble, thinking of others as better than
yourselves. Don't look out only for your own
interests, but take an interest in others, too.
PHILIPPIANS 2:3–4 NLT

We were struggling with selfishness in our house for a season. One of our family members in particular needed a character lesson in this area. As I was praying over the situation, I felt prompted to call one of our favorite teachers for advice. She loved both of my kids and knew them well. She also loved Jesus. So she was the perfect go-to for specific and wise counsel.

I explained the situation and asked what she thought. She had a great idea. She said to have this particular child put on a pair of shoes that were a size or two too small for them and have them wear them for the day. Their feet would feel uncomfortable and pinched all day long. Then let them know that this is what others around them feel like when they act selfishly.

Now, to tell the truth, we didn't have a pair of smaller shoes to carry out this exercise, but we did discuss the idea at length with the child. And every time selfishness started rearing its ugly head in our house, we brought up the idea of pinched toes. We remember it to this day.

Selfishness is a big problem. And if we're honest with

ourselves, we probably struggle with it more than we'd ever admit to anyone. I was being selfish with my son recently, wanting him to do something for me right then and there when he was in the middle of something that was important to him. My thing could wait. I remembered that I was probably causing him to feel some pinched toes with my own selfishness.

First Corinthians 10:24 (AMP) says, "Let no one seek [only] his own good, but [also] that of the other person." Another friend we know has her kids practice this at home. They take turns letting the other family members go first so that when they are in school or away from home, they won't be selfish there either.

If you struggle with selfishness, it's time to do something about it. Before you find some old shoes and start walking around in them, repent and ask Jesus for help. Confess your sin of selfishness to Him and allow the Holy Spirit to dig out that ugly root. Ask Him to plant more fruits of His Spirit instead. Can you picture that as you pray?

Jesus, I repent of my selfishness. I need help here. Would You dig out the roots of selfishness and plant something new there instead? Please grow love, joy, peace, patience, kindness, goodness, faithfulness, gentleness, and self-control in me.

TAKING A REST

By the seventh day God had finished the work he had been doing; so on the seventh day he rested from all his work. Then God blessed the seventh day and made it holy, because on it he rested from all the work of creating that he had done.

GENESIS 2:2–3 NIV

My husband flies back and forth to Colorado frequently for work. The last time he was at the airport, his first flight was delayed by two hours. Instead of arriving around lunchtime in Colorado like he was supposed to, his flight didn't get in until around 9:00 p.m. It was a long day of flying and rearranging flights. He was in five different airports that day trying to get where he needed to go. He found out that the reason his first flight was delayed was that the Federal Aviation Administration (FAA) has specific rules about how much sleep a crew needs to have before they can fly again. The crew hadn't had enough rest, so they were grounded until they got what they needed.

Rest is very important. Your body needs a specific amount of sleep to be healthy. If you keep waking up feeling exhausted, your body isn't getting enough. Talk to your parents about how you can manage your sleep habits better. Staying up too late on a regular basis is not good for your health.

It's also important to rest from things that cause you stress. We make it a habit at our house to spend less time on electronic devices on Sundays. Smartphones, social media, and news often cause us stress. We turn off the ringers and only use our phones occasionally on Sunday afternoons. What causes you stress? Take a few minutes and make a list of things that cause you stress. Is it possible to rearrange your schedule so that one day a week can be a day of rest and relaxation? It was important to God to rest after His work, and He did that so we would follow His example. Ask God to help you rearrange things so that you can rest from stressful things and enjoy worshipping him and having fun with friends and family every week.

Mark 2:27–28 (NLT) says, "Then Jesus said to them, 'The Sabbath was made to meet the needs of people, and not people to meet the requirements of the Sabbath. So the Son of Man is Lord, even over the Sabbath!' "

In Matthew 11:28–30, Jesus tells us to come to Him and rest. He is the source of life, and as we rest in Him, He fills us up to be and do all that He created us for.

Jesus, I come to You as my source of life and rest.
Help me rearrange my schedule so that I can unplug
from things that cause me stress and focus on You.

WHEN TRAGEDY STRIKES

*The Lord is close to the brokenhearted and
saves those who are crushed in spirit.*
PSALM 34:18 NIV

❋

This morning at our church, it was announced that a seven-teen-year-old boy, a member of our church's youth group, was killed in a tragic car accident over the weekend. The families and students who knew him are grieving deeply. It's hard to make sense of it all. One of the youth pastors prayed and asked for God's comfort to come and that somehow this tragedy would be used to further God's kingdom.

Isaiah 55:8–9 (NLT) says, " 'My thoughts are nothing like your thoughts,' says the Lord. 'And my ways are far beyond anything you could imagine. For just as the heavens are higher than the earth, so my ways are higher than your ways and my thoughts higher than your thoughts.' "

As Christians, we can trust that God's ways are better than we could ever imagine. God promises in Matthew 5:4 to bless and comfort those who mourn. But still we grieve. We don't under-stand why some things happen the way they do. We doubt. We want to point fingers. Waves of emotions take us through many stages of grief. Psychologists have identified several different stages that people who are grieving go through, including denial, anger, guilt, depression, and acceptance. Death seems so final and completely out of our control. We want answers.

A good friend of ours lost her husband to cancer when she

was in her early twenties. She had two young boys. Her husband had recently committed his life to Christ before his diagnosis, and during that time he had shared the hope and love and freedom in Christ he'd found with others. His sister came to trust and follow Jesus before his death. She said that her brother's illness is what woke her up to the reality of Jesus Christ. She, in turn, has raised her children to know and love Jesus. Her brother's life made a difference in his generation and the next because of his faith in Christ.

As believers in Jesus Christ, we have this hope found in 1 Corinthians 15:54–55, 57 (NLT): "Then, when our dying bodies have been transformed into bodies that will never die, this Scripture will be fulfilled: 'Death is swallowed up in victory. O death, where is your victory? O death, where is your sting?'.... But thank God! He gives us victory over sin and death through our Lord Jesus Christ."

Death is not the end. We put our hope in Christ alone.

Jesus, thank You that I'm alive in You. Thank You that death is not the end. You have conquered death, and one day everything will be made right again. I put all my hope and all my trust in You. You are good, and I love You.

POPULARITY CONTEST

*"Ask, and it will be given to you; seek, and you
will find; knock, and it will be opened to you."*
MATTHEW 7:7 ESV

Kristy had always wanted to direct a play that would make a
difference in the lives of teenagers. She was young, but she was
talented and had some experience in drama and leadership. She
believed that God was planting this dream in her heart, and she
felt called to do it. The time was right for a decision to be made.
She prayed and asked God to open doors. She prayed for the
right contacts to make. She prayed for the right people to help
her. She prayed for the students who would have roles in this
play. She received a lot of green lights and open doors. She
contacted tons of families and teens in her area. There was a
great response to the interest form she created and emailed to
everyone on her list. The time came for auditions.

The day of auditions arrived, the leaders met and prayed,
parents volunteered to help with registration, but only a few
students trickled in to audition. Then a few more came. And a
few more. There were barely enough people to fill up the cast
list. Kristy was disappointed when several people who said they
would be there didn't show. She had to remind herself that this
event was prayed over and that she believed she was doing
what God asked her to do. This was not a popularity contest.
The response of the students who didn't come did not change
Kristy's worth or value in the eyes of God. She decided then and

there not to take it personally.

Kristy took a deep breath and gave God her fears and worries. She began to trust that God handpicked who would be in this play. He had a purpose for bringing the people together who showed up. He was building a team, and it would be a good one. She clapped her hands together and shared with the students how loved and valued they were. And that God had brought them all together for His special purpose.

Taking things personally and feeling offended or left out can cause a ripple of emotions to surface. You have a choice with what to do with those feelings. You can bring them to Jesus and align yourself with His love, His truth, and His kingdom purpose, or you can let them fester.

Festering feelings can cause all sorts of problems. The next time you feel that urge to take something personally and get offended, go to Jesus first. You are not in a popularity contest. Your position as a daughter of the King is secure. And His plans for you are good, no matter how many people show up!

God, thank You that You are always speaking love and truth over my life. I'm thankful to be loved and valued by You no matter what anyone else thinks or says or does!

BRAIN FOG

Set your minds on things above, not on earthly things.
COLOSSIANS 3:2 NIV

"Okay, class, let's put on our thinking caps!" Have you ever heard a teacher say that? I heard this many times in my school while growing up, specifically when the "specials" teacher came to visit every few months. She led our class in brainstorming games in which we learned critical thinking skills and how to think "outside the box."

Thinking wisely and critically is a skill you learn to develop as you mature. But Lauren was really struggling in that department. She liked staying up late and felt like her brain worked better at nighttime, so that's when she worked on her homework. Mornings were rough. She had a hard time turning on her brain, and she realized she often made poor choices in the morning—forgetting things, being grumpy with her family members, forgetting to let the dog out, and more. She was in a fog until midday. And she didn't seem to care about it until her mom let her know that her attitude and forgetfulness were causing problems with the rest of the family.

The Bible tells us to "set our minds on things above." Setting our minds brings up the idea of setting a clock or a watch or a timer. You set it to the right time, and you expect it to stay that way, to alert you to do what you set it for. But that takes a specific action on your part. Your timer isn't going to set itself. You must specifically set it to go off automatically every day.

Let's take a look at today's verse in a few different versions and see what kind of solutions we can come up with:

* "Set your mind and keep focused habitually on the things above [the heavenly things], not on things that are on the earth [which have only temporal value" (AMP).

* "So if you're serious about living this new resurrection life with Christ, act like it. Pursue the things over which Christ presides. Don't shuffle along, eyes to the ground, absorbed with the things right in front of you. Look up, and be alert to what is going on around Christ—that's where the action is. See things from his perspective" (MSG).

"Keep focused habitually."
"Don't shuffle along. . . . Look up!"

Lauren had some choices to make. She loved God and wanted to honor Him with her heart and mind. She asked for help and began changing her schedule. She started her homework earlier in the evening. She went to bed thirty minutes earlier than usual. And when she woke up, she started her day with prayer, "setting her mind" on Jesus and His kingdom.

Lord, help me set my mind on You before I start my day!

183

JESUS IS THE ONLY WAY

"Enter through the narrow gate. For wide is the gate and broad is the road that leads to destruction, and many enter through it. But small is the gate and narrow the road that leads to life, and only a few find it."
MATTHEW 7:13–14 NIV

When I was a teenager, I went on a mission trip for an entire summer with a large group of high school students from all over the United States. We went to several states, sharing the love of Jesus through songs, stories, puppet shows for kids, service projects, and more. The trip was full of life-changing moments and was a summer I'll never forget. One of the songs we sang, with puppets on our hands, was about walking the straight and narrow path God has for us. It was a fun and quirky song with a catchy tune that I can still remember thirty years later. Songs are good like that. They can take an important concept and shorten it into a three-minute song that you remember for a lifetime. This little song shared a major truth from God's Word.

In John 10:7–9 (NLT), Jesus says, "I tell you the truth, I am the gate for the sheep. All who came before me were thieves and robbers. But the true sheep did not listen to them. Yes, I am the gate. Those who come in through me will be saved. They will come and go freely and will find good pastures."

Jesus is the Way and the Truth and the Life (John 14:6). You will never regret following Him through the narrow gate into eternal life. That life begins now and goes throughout all eternity.

I was talking with a friend recently, and she said that someone in her family had their home broken into. She said her family member loved God, though, and that his response to the robber was probably "Do you want to know about Jesus?" That's an extreme example, but wouldn't the world change for the better if more of us would respond to difficult situations with the love and hope of Jesus on our minds? He is the narrow gate, the only way to eternal life with God in heaven.

So whether you're sharing that news to children with puppets on your hands or witnessing to criminals or something in between, God has a message—"the" message—for you to share with the world. Not only with your words but with your life and your actions.

Lord Jesus, I want to love You with my whole life. Let my words and actions spread Your love into the world. Please give me boldness as I talk with others about the way You can change anyone's life who chooses to follow the narrow path.

TOO MUCH OF A GOOD THING?

If you find honey, eat just enough—
too much of it, and you will vomit.
PROVERBS 25:16 NIV

What a proverb, huh? Our family has experienced this personally in several interesting ways. First, we went on vacation and ordered a dessert called "The Kitchen Sink." This dessert was shared by four of us and contained eight scoops of ice cream, cookies, brownies, candy bars, one full can of whipped cream, and, as the menu stated, was "smothered in every additional topping we have." This thing was every kid's dream. It came in a huge bowl that looked like a kitchen sink. We all dug in. One of us ate more than the others. And we soon found out who that was because that person spent a few hours in the bathroom throwing it all right back up.

The second time we experienced this as a family was when my husband's friend sent us a freezer full of salmon he had caught in Alaska. We were cooking salmon often. Grilling it. Baking it. Topping it with specialty sauces. Putting it in a salad. It was so yummy and fresh—better than any we'd tasted before. But we kept eating it. And making it again. And eating more. Now some of us can't even stand the thought of salmon anymore. We just had too much of a good thing.

Have you experienced too much of a good thing? Maybe

its social media. You're not doing anything wrong on there, just spending too much time. Maybe you have trouble keeping your hands out of the cookie jar. Maybe you have trouble stopping when you're playing video games. Maybe you binge-watch too many shows.

When I was young, I was part of a small group of young adults who thought it would be a good experiment to see if we could hang out every single night for a month. It was fun at first. We studied the Bible. Prayed. Played games. Ate food. Sang songs. Stayed up too late. We did it again the next night. Whoever could come came. We did it again and again until nearly thirty days had passed. By the end of the month, many of us were exhausted and sick because we had passed a cold around from one to another.

The Bible tells us that it's possible to have too much of a good thing. Today's Proverb reminds us to be wise in how much of something we consume. Is this hitting home for you? Is there anything you're consuming too much of right now? Let's pray about that.

Jesus, I give You permission to highlight anything in me that needs some work. Point out ways that I'm consuming too much, even if it's something good. I know You want me healthy. I want that too. Help me to know when enough is enough.

PLANNING AHEAD

"Is there anyone here who, planning to build a new house, doesn't first sit down and figure the cost so you'll know if you can complete it? If you only get the foundation laid and then run out of money, you're going to look pretty foolish. Everyone passing by will poke fun at you: 'He started something he couldn't finish.'"

LUKE 14:28 MSG

Jake and Jessa are talented artists. They've been taking art lessons for years. Jake is a cartoon artist. He likes to create comic books, and he has a funny way of adding conversation to his artwork. Jessa is a traditional artist. She is skilled in drawing and using chalk and paints. Her animal drawings really come to life on the page. Both kids have learned the importance of planning ahead in their artwork.

Jake found out the hard way that if he didn't plan how many boxes he would need to have in his cartoon, part of his comic would get cut off. The same was true for the conversation happening inside those little boxes. The words needed to fit. Jessa learned that if she didn't lightly sketch out her drawing ahead of time before adding paint, she often ran off the edges of the paper.

Planning ahead is something you won't regret. And not planning ahead is something you definitely will. Proverbs 13:16 (NLT) says, "Wise people think before they act; fools don't—and even brag about their foolishness."

Planning ahead takes wisdom and prayer. Remember Proverbs 16:9? It says, "We can make our plans, but the Lord determines our steps" (NLT). It's really important to invite Jesus into your planning. He has special plans and purposes for your life. And if you're planning something that goes in a different direction than what He has for you, that's going to be a waste of your time and resources.

Before you begin planning, ask God for wisdom. Is this the direction He has for you? Allow Him to lead you. Watch as He opens and shuts doors. Are you planning something important, like which high school classes to take to get into college? Prayerfully consider all the options. Ask for peace. Planning something small like a party or artwork or an outfit to wear? God cares about all that too. He loves to be a part of everything about you.

God gives us freedom to make all kinds of choices in life. So don't let choosing the wrong thing paralyze you. Move forward in the direction that gives you peace, and trust that if you're going the wrong way, the Holy Spirit will make it clear to you.

Lord, thanks for caring about the things I care about. I want to get better at planning ahead and inviting You into my decision-making. Help me make wise decisions as I grow up.

A GOOD EXAMPLE

The integrity of the upright guides them.
PROVERBS 11:3 ESV

We've talked about being faithful in the small stuff. The older you get, the more you'll realize that the small stuff adds up and becomes the big stuff. When you're faithful in small things, especially when no one is looking, you're starting to grow up and mature into a devoted follower of Christ. You're becoming a person of integrity.

You've probably heard this before, but spiritual maturity has very little to do with age. Grown adults have trouble with integrity and maturity. (If you spend five minutes on social media, you realize this quickly.) It's been said that integrity is who you are when no one is looking. Are you faithful in the small things? You can be a great example, even to adults! First Timothy 4:12 (NIV) says, "Don't let anyone look down on you because you are young, but set an example for the believers in speech, in conduct, in love, in faith and in purity."

Matthew 18:2–4 (AMP) says, "He called a little child and set him before them, and said, 'I assure you and most solemnly say to you, unless you repent [that is, change your inner self—your old way of thinking, live changed lives] and become like children [trusting, humble, and forgiving], you will never enter the kingdom of heaven. Therefore, whoever humbles himself like this child is greatest in the kingdom of heaven.' "

It seems that children love and forgive a lot easier than

grown-ups do. They also tend to have an easier time hearing from God than adults do. Children can teach us a lot about faith. Sometimes kids get it right more than adults do, and we can learn from them.

Cassie was younger than nearly everyone else in the room, but God gave her a message, and she showed up. Her insides were quaking and many eyeballs were on her, but God gave her strength and empowered her to speak truth to the crowd. She felt judgment at first, like she wasn't old enough to inform them about anything. But as she shared what God had done in her life, the atmosphere shifted and God's Word did its job.

God's Word says not to let anyone look down on you for being young. You are right where God has you for a reason. You bring something important to the table. God can use you greatly in the lives of others. Don't be afraid to lead or speak out if God has given you something to say. You are very valuable in the kingdom!

Lord, thank You for loving me and telling me about my worth. Help me to be a good example, even to older people. Help me love and serve You humbly. Give me courage to share my story about what You're doing in and through my life.

191

SNAKES IN THE YARD

*"The thief comes only in order to steal and kill and
destroy. I came that they may have and enjoy life, and
have it in abundance [to the full, till it overflows]."*
JOHN 10:10 AMP

Our house is surrounded by cornfields on one side and woods
on the other. It's a lovely setting, and we enjoy it very much. But
being out in the country with those surroundings comes with
quite a bit of wildlife. We see a plethora of deer, wild turkeys, raccoons, ground squirrels, tree squirrels, cardinals, hummingbirds,
and much more. But it also comes with a lot of less desirable
wildlife too—namely, snakes.

The first time I saw one, I squealed. Thankfully, they seem
mostly to be harmless garter snakes. But one time, we found a
larger snake in the shed that a neighbor told us could be poisonous. Just looking up the images online to determine what
kind of snake it was gave me the heebie-jeebies! Ugh!

Being outside brings us all joy, but I have to admit that the
snakes in the yard caused me to reconsider my love for the out-
doors. My daughter stepped on a snake once in her bare feet. It
totally freaked her out! The snakes also like to hide in my favorite
flowers: lily of the valley. I went to pick some one day, and out
slithered a snake. But instead of letting the snakes rob our joy, we
just learned to wear shoes or bring our dog Daisy along wherever
we go. Daisy is really good at sniffing out the snakes, killing them,
and then (for some extremely weird reason) rolling on them.

The snakes in our yard remind me of today's verse. Jesus says that our enemy comes to steal, kill, and destroy. The snakes were threatening to steal our joy of the beautiful creation we live in. But Jesus came so that we could have an abundant and full life, now and for all eternity.

Take a minute and ask God to reveal anything in your life that is stealing your joy. Maybe the "snakes in your yard" could be a friendship that tends toward gossip or unhealthy peer pressure. Maybe having too many activities and commitments is robbing you of joy. Maybe you are believing lies about yourself or God.

If you feel like you have a situation in life that is robbing you of joy, talk to Jesus about it. Tell Him how you feel, and allow Him to bring His abundant life back into your situation.

Jesus, I need Your abundant life to come in and roll over the snakes in my life that are stealing my joy!

THE FREAK OCTOBER SNOWSTORM

Those who live in the shelter of the Most High will find rest in the shadow of the Almighty. This I declare about the LORD: He alone is my refuge, my place of safety; he is my God, and I trust him.
PSALM 91:1–2 NLT

We were coming home from class one afternoon in late October. Suddenly, it got very cold outside. The clouds were full, and they swiftly erupted with huge flakes of soggy snow. Slush lined the streets, and the roads became slippery fast. We started to slow down. Behind us, I could see a minivan coming at us very quickly. It was not slowing down. I turned my signal on and tried to turn off the main highway onto a back road, but my tires were spinning and we were sliding. Even though we were going very slowly, I slid past the road I wanted to turn onto. The minivan was upon us, and sure enough, they ran right into us. The driver had also tried to slow down but couldn't. Thankfully, no one was hurt.

What happened next was like a scene from a movie. I got out to assess the damage and get insurance information from the other driver. We were pulled off on the side of a busy road. Cars and trucks kept speeding by. I went to get back into my car, and a large truck went through a puddle right next to me. I was covered in slush from head to toe.

I regret a lot of things about that day, but sometimes bad days just happen. And God can use them for good. As we waited for the state highway patrol to appear, my nearly sixteen-year-old son (who would soon be taking driver's ed) got to experience what it was like to be in an accident and what to do about it. And glory be to God, he was able to have that real-life experience without anyone being injured. We both learned to be more careful on these rural roads and to expect rapid weather changes in this new state we lived in. Then when I got home, my husband gave me a big hug and took care of dinner so that I could have a rest.

Some days, you just need to be held by someone you love—and a hot bath doesn't hurt either. When I look back on that day, I see some life lessons for sure. But what I remember most is the love I felt from just being held.

God is always with us to bring comfort in just the right way.

Lord, thank You for being with me always.
You provide exactly what I need when I need
it. You are my shelter and my place of safety.
Thank You for the love and comfort
of friends and family too.

TAKING CARE OF YOU

*Do you not know that your bodies are temples of the
Holy Spirit, who is in you, whom you have received
from God? You are not your own; you were bought
at a price. Therefore honor God with your bodies.*
1 CORINTHIANS 6:19–20 NIV

Do you know anyone who has developed a chronic illness later
in life? One thing you may hear someone like that say is that
they wish they'd taken better care of their body when they were
younger. We know a few people who have regrets like that. They
wish they hadn't smoked all their life. They wish they hadn't
done drugs. They wish they hadn't eaten all that sugar and junk
food. All those choices have a way of creeping up on a person.
Months turn into years, years turn into decades, and before you
know it, the consequences of those choices can't be undone:
Lung cancer. Alzheimer's disease. Obesity. Heart attack.

It's easy to think you're invincible when you're young. You
have your whole life to make better choices. But that is foolish
thinking.

The good news is that no matter what kind of regrets you
have and no matter how old you are, God's grace and love cover
you! First Peter 4:8 (NIV) tells us that "love covers over a multitude of sins." And 1 John 1:9 (NIV) says, "If we confess our sins,
he is faithful and just and will forgive us our sins and purify us
from all unrighteousness."

You may have natural consequences for poor choices, but

God can make your heart brand-new. And He can renew your health too. Check this out: "He gives power to the weak and strength to the powerless. Even youths will become weak and tired, and young men will fall in exhaustion. But those who trust in the LORD will find new strength. They will soar high on wings like eagles. They will run and not grow weary. They will walk and not faint" (Isaiah 40:29–31 NLT).

Your body is a temple of the Holy Spirit. Read that again! Your body is the place where God chooses to dwell. So take care of your body, friend. It's important. Learn what foods are healthy and what treats to enjoy only on special occasions. The Bible talks about times to feast and times to fast. Pay attention in health class, and learn how God designed your body to work and what it needs to run best. That way you'll have no regrets with your health.

Lord, I'm thankful for this body You gave me. Help me treat it well and learn what's good for me and what could be harmful in the long run. I know my body is Your temple. Help me to honor You in my body and make good choices with my foods and my activities.

TRANSFORMING YOUR EVERYDAY LIFE

*Do not conform to the pattern of this world, but be
transformed by the renewing of your mind. Then
you will be able to test and approve what God's
will is—his good, pleasing and perfect will.*
ROMANS 12:2 NIV

The Message says Romans 12:1–2 this way: "So here's what I want you to do, God helping you: Take your everyday, ordinary life—your sleeping, eating, going-to-work, and walking-around life—and place it before God as an offering. Embracing what God does for you is the best thing you can do for him. Don't become so well-adjusted to your culture that you fit into it without even thinking. Instead, fix your attention on God. You'll be changed from the inside out. Readily recognize what he wants from you, and quickly respond to it. Unlike the culture around you, always dragging you down to its level of immaturity, God brings the best out of you, develops well-formed maturity in you." *The Message* paraphrase gives us a visual picture we can apply to our lives. Let's break this down:

First, with God's help, take everything you do, including sleeping, eating, going to school, everything about you and your life, "and place it before God as an offering." Make this your prayer today. Can you imagine this as you close your eyes? Begin your prayer and picture giving everything about you and your life to Jesus as an offering.

Next, embrace what God does for you. Invite Him in to change you from the inside out. Fix your full attention on Him. Get rid of any distractions.

Now ask God to reveal anything going on in You that is not honoring to Him. Ask Him to reveal ways that you've become too much like the culture around you. Are you indistinguishable as a follower of Jesus? Ask God to convict your heart in areas that need a renewal. Humble yourself before God and allow Him to do some cleanup work in your heart. When the Holy Spirit convicts your heart, it will be clean. He won't smother you with shame. He'll highlight what He wants you to be aware of, you confess it and repent, and His grace covers you and gives you power to go another direction.

Can you picture fresh water flowing through you as God cleans up the areas in your heart that need tending? What does that feel like? Spend time praising God for His love, His grace, His care, and His mighty power for you.

Prayers like this one can transform your everyday life. Make it a habit!

Lord, please renew my mind today. Wash me clean in Your living water and change my heart and mind to conform with Yours. Transform me by the power of Your Spirit who is alive and at work in me.

NOTHIN' TO PROVE

Fearing people is a dangerous trap,
but trusting the LORD means safety.
PROVERBS 29:25 NLT

Miranda has a beautiful singing voice. God gave her that gift to use for His glory. She sang for church and events and parties. But as she grew older, some friends became critical of her and her voice. She heard them talking behind her back. They said unkind things, maybe out of jealousy. They said she was a show-off. That hurt. Miranda let their words get to her, and she stopped singing in public.

When the Bible talks about "fearing people" or "the fear of man," it's talking about being more concerned about what other people think of you than of what God thinks of you. This is a common problem, even in churches and ministries. Leaders are often concerned about what their followers think of them—so much so that it disables them from doing what God is calling them to do.

Miranda went through a time of deep healing when God became real to her. She began to ask herself questions like the ones we see in Galatians 1:10 (NIV): "Am I now trying to win the approval of human beings, or of God? Or am I trying to please people? If I were still trying to please people, I would not be a servant of Christ."

Miranda realized that God loved her deeply and gifted her for a purpose. He was the one she wanted to please with her life.

She finally figured out that she had nothing to prove to anyone anymore. She could sing for God's glory alone. She knew who she was in Christ, and that was enough.

Just like Miranda, you are loved and gifted for a purpose too. God calls each of us to serve Him in ways that bring Him glory, no matter what other people think or say. It won't be easy. People might even say some mean things behind your back. But God is bigger than all of that. And His power is what is working inside you. Check it out:

Ephesians 1:19–21 (NLT) says, "I also pray that you will understand the incredible greatness of God's power for us who believe him. This is the same mighty power that raised Christ from the dead and seated him in the place of honor at God's right hand in the heavenly realms. Now he is far above any ruler or authority or power or leader or anything else—not only in this world but also in the world to come."

Lord, You are bigger than any power or leader or person's opinion that I might be afraid of. In You, I have nothing to lose and everything to gain. Thank You, Jesus!

GOOD THINKING!

Finally, brothers and sisters, whatever is true, whatever is noble, whatever is right, whatever is pure, whatever is lovely, whatever is admirable—if anything is excellent or praiseworthy—think about such things. Whatever you have learned or received or heard from me, or seen in me—put it into practice. And the God of peace will be with you.

PHILIPPIANS 4:8–9 NIV

We have a plaque on our wall that says, "Change your thoughts and you will change your world." I don't know who wrote it, but it is something to think about (see what I did there?)!

It has also been said that "you are what you think." It's clear that what you think about is pretty important. Your thoughts lead to beliefs and actions—sometimes in a dozen different directions. And it's easy to regret where you let your thoughts lead you.

Christian counselor Kevin Ness uses this example when talking about the thought life: Close your eyes and picture a swirling tornado. Which direction is it swirling in your mind? Okay, now stop and make the tornado swirl in the opposite direction. Can you picture all of that in your mind? Great! It shows that you can "take your thoughts captive." You can control your thoughts. You can make your thoughts obedient to Christ (2 Corinthians 10:5).

If you have a long list of regrets, it's easy to get down on yourself. It's easy to feel shame over past mistakes. It's easy to wallow in despair and discouragement. If you're looking for easy,

easy often leads down the road of more regret.

But moving forward after experiencing regret and failure takes courage and strength from God. Paul, in Philippians 3:13–14 (NLT), tells us what's important: "I focus on this one thing: Forgetting the past and looking forward to what lies ahead, I press on to reach the end of the race and receive the heavenly prize for which God, through Christ Jesus, is calling us."

What's getting in the way of your thought life? Is it too much screen time and social media where other people are telling you what to think? Is it believing lies about yourself? Is it feeling shame over past mistakes? Is it fear of more failure?

Bring all of these to Jesus in prayer. Picture yourself laying them all down one by one. Ask Jesus what He wants you to know as you bring Him your list of regrets.

Lord Jesus, please take my list of regrets and failures. I let go of them. I don't want them to taint my heart and mind anymore. Let Your Spirit work in my mind to take my thoughts captive and make them obedient to You. Help me think good thoughts instead of rehearsing my list of failures. Help me move forward into the life You've called me to.

A NO-REGRETS LIFE

*Now may the God of peace make you holy in every way,
and may your whole spirit and soul and body be kept
blameless until our Lord Jesus Christ comes again. God
will make this happen, for he who calls you is faithful.*
1 THESSALONIANS 5:23–24 NLT

The Message says it this way: "May God himself, the God who makes everything holy and whole, make you holy and whole, put you together—spirit, soul, and body—and keep you fit for the coming of our Master, Jesus Christ. The One who called you is completely dependable. If he said it, he'll do it!"

If you've had some regrets in your life, you can trust that God is working everything together for your good. How do you know that's true? Because Romans 8:28 (NIV) tells us this: "We know that in all things God works for the good of those who love him, who have been called according to his purpose."

You can believe it. Count on it. God is putting you together "spirit, soul, and body." He is completely dependable. Take a look at how the Amplified Bible translates today's verse: "Now may the God of peace Himself sanctify you through and through [that is, separate you from profane and vulgar things, make you pure and whole and undamaged—consecrated to Him—set apart for His purpose]; and may your spirit and soul and body be kept complete and [be found] blameless at the coming of our Lord Jesus Christ. Faithful and absolutely trustworthy is He who is calling you [to Himself for your salvation], and He will do it [He will fulfill His call by making you holy, guarding you, watching over you, and protecting you as His own]" (1 Thessalonians 5:23–24 AMP).

God is faithful and absolutely trustworthy! Only He has the power to make you pure and holy, to put you back together "whole and undamaged." That's right, "whole and undamaged." Even if you've messed up so much that you don't feel like trying again. Even if your list of regrets is longer than it has ever been. God is working out all the details of your life and creating a masterpiece with you. Let Him have His way in your heart. Let Him get in there and help you sort things out.

God is "guarding you, watching over you, and protecting you" because You're His kid and He loves you beyond measure. As you walk with Him day by day, listening for His voice and walking in His ways, you can live a no-regrets life.

Trust God to do what He said He will do. You won't ever regret it!

I love You, God. I trust that You are making me new—whole and undamaged. Help me walk with You daily so that I can live a no-regrets life.

SCRIPTURE INDEX

OLD TESTAMENT

NEW TESTAMENT